TOP 10
COPENHAGEN

ANTONIA CUNNINGHAM

Penguin
Random
House

Top 10 Copenhagen Highlights

The Top 10 of Everything

CONTENTS

Copenhagen Area by Area

Streetsmart

Within each Top 10 list in this book, no hierarchy of quality or popularity is implied. All 10 are, in the editor's opinion, of roughly equal merit.

Front cover and spine The famously colourful waterfront of Nyhavn
Back cover Tivoli's Moorish palace twinkles with Christmas lights
Title page Gefionspringvandet, named after the Norse goddess who created the local land

Welcome to
Copenhagen

Welcome to Copenhagen, the cultural capital of northern Europe and birthplace of hygge. A charming, compact city where opulent palaces stand shoulder to shoulder with modern architectural masterpieces, the Danish capital can be experienced in a multitude of different ways. With Eyewitness Top 10 Copenhagen, it's yours to explore.

Copenhagen has royal credentials that are clear the moment you set foot on the city's cobblestone streets, with magnificent palaces, castles and churches dominating the skyline. But even with its regal past (it's home to the world's oldest monarchy) casting a long shadow, Copenhagen remains a dynamic, modern city with much to offer even the most museum-wary traveller – from world-class restaurants, hip nightlife and high-end boutiques to breathtaking parks, urban beaches and cosy cafés.

It's no coincidence that Denmark is often cited as the happiest nation on earth. Danes may be direct – and their humour dry – but they know better than most how to enjoy the finer things in life. After all, hygge – the Danish lifestyle trend that loosely translates into a feeling of warmth and cosiness – is now almost as popular outside of Denmark as one of the country's other great exports: beer.

Whether you're visiting for a weekend or a week, our Top 10 guide brings together the best of everything the city has to offer, from vibrant **Vesterbro** to stately **Slotsholmen** and beyond. The guide gives you useful tips throughout, from seeking out what's free to avoiding the crowds, plus seven easy-to-follow itineraries, designed to tie together a clutch of sights in a short space of time. Add inspiring photography and detailed maps, and you've got the essential pocket-sized travel companion. **Enjoy the book, and enjoy Copenhagen.**

Clockwise from top: **Christiansborg Slot**, the interior of Grundtvigs Kirke, houses on Nyhavn, the Frederiksborg Slot gardens, ceiling of Marmorkirken dome, Amalienborg sentries, street art in Christiania

Exploring Copenhagen

Copenhagen may not be the biggest of capital cities, but it punches well above its weight in terms of culture, history and charm. Despite its compact size, there is a lot to see and do. To help you make the most of your visit, here are some ideas for a two- or four-day trip.

Christiansborg Slot has magnificent interiors.

Key
— Two-day itinerary
— Four-day itinerary

Nyhavn is a waterfront entertainment area.

Two Days in Copenhagen

Day ❶

MORNING

Set sail from **Nyhavn** *(see pp22–3)* on a canal tour, then stroll along the promenade past the Royal Danish Playhouse. Follow the harbourside path until you reach **Amalienborg** *(see pp24–5)*, where you can watch the changing of the guard. Have lunch at **Kompasset** *(see p75)*.

AFTERNOON

Head west on Gothersgade until you reach **Kongens Have** *(see pp16–17)*. Stroll through the gardens, then continue to **Rosenborg Slot** *(see pp16–17)* to see the crown jewels. Walk north on Øster Voldgade and visit **Statens Museum for Kunst** *(see pp26–7)*, finishing the afternoon by having a drink at **Torvehallerne KBH** *(see p63)*.

Day ❷

MORNING

Begin the day at **Nationalmuseet** *(see pp30–31)*, making sure to visit the Viking exhibition. Next, go to **Slotsholmen** *(see pp32–3)* and visit the Royal Stables before taking a tour of the Royal Reception Rooms at Christiansborg Slot. Climb the palace tower for amazing views. Stop at the Tower Restaurant for an innovative spin on a *smørrebrød* (open sandwich).

AFTERNOON

Head southwest on Stormgade to **Ny Carlsberg Glyptotek** *(see p70)*, before crossing Tietgensgade and exploring **Tivoli** *(see pp14–15)*. After spending a couple of hours here, exit onto Vesterbrogade and walk east towards the **Latin Quarter** *(see pp18–19)* for sightseeing and shops.

Four Days in Copenhagen

Day ❶

MORNING

Start the day with a visit to **Statens Museum for Kunst** *(see pp26–7)*, then cross Georg Brandes Plads and make your way to **Rosenborg Slot** *(see pp16–17)*. Take a guided tour of

Day ❸
MORNING
Start the day with a trip to **Zoologisk Have** (see p88), and visit the elephant house here. Stroll through **Frederiksberg Have** (see p87) before exiting onto Pile Alle. Pass under the elephant gate and into the **Carlsberg Brewery** (see p88).
AFTERNOON
Stroll northeast and stop at **Bakkehusmuseet** (see p89). Turn right onto Vesterbrogade and call in at **WestMarket** (see p89) for a late lunch. Continue on Vesterbrogade and turn right onto Gasværksvej, following the road until you reach Kødbyen, where you will find a plethora of trendy bars.

Day ❹
MORNING
Begin the day with a coffee at one of the many cafés along Studiestræde before exploring into the bustling **Latin Quarter** (see pp18–19). Head up Store Kannikestræde to Rundtårn, and then hike to the top. Continue into **Nyhavn** (see pp22–3) for lunch.
AFTERNOON
Take a boat tour of the canals and jump off at **Holmens Kirke** (see p41). Walk west along Gammel Strand, passing **Rådhus** (see p70) before turning onto Vesterbrogade. Take a left into **Tivoli** (see pp14–15), and spend the afternoon wandering the beautiful 19th-century pleasure gardens.

the 17th-century palace before exiting into **Kongens Have** (see pp16–17). Head east to **Marmorkirken**, and then on to **Amalienborg** (see pp24–5). Stop at **Ida Davidsen** (see p83) for lunch.
AFTERNOON
Walk west, stopping to admire the Gefionspringvandet and St Alban's Church before crossing the footbridge into **Kastellet** (see p80). See the **Little Mermaid** (see p80) from the fortress ramparts, then catch a 1A bus into **Kongens Nytorv** (see pp22–3). Stroll along Strøget, then have a drink at one of Amagertorv's cafés.

Day ❷
MORNING
Start the day at **Nationalmuseet** (see pp30–31) and museum-hop on **Slotsholmen** (see pp32–3) before popping into the Royal Stables. Take a torchlit tour of the ruins under Christiansborg Slot.
AFTERNOON
Cross the **harbour** (see pp12–13) and enter Christianshavn. Turn right to visit the **Christians Kirke** (see p93) on Strandgade, then head east until you reach the canal, crossing the bridge on Sankt Annæ Gade and arrive at **Vor Frelsers Kirke** (see p94). Spend the afternoon in **Christiania** (see pp28–9).

Tivoli Gardens has manicured lawns, flowers and fountains.

Top 10 Copenhagen Highlights

Fishing boats on the water in the historic district of Nyhavn

Copenhagen Highlights

Copenhagen is a vibrant city offering an array of experiences. Walk through the cobbled streets of the medieval city, explore world-class museums, experience the finest restaurants and hippest nightlife, or simply unwind beside the gorgeous waters of one of the nearby peaceful seaside towns. This charming destination has something for everyone.

1 Harbour Sights

The best way to soak up Copenhagen's harbour sights is to take a boat trip along the canals of Slotsholmen and Christianshavn. It is also a good way to understand the city's development *(see pp12–13)*.

2 Tivoli

This pleasure garden and funfair attracts kids and adults. The rides are great for an adrenaline rush, and if you feel peckish there are many restaurants *(see pp14–15)*.

3 Rosenborg Slot and Kongens Have

Set in one of the city's prettiest parks, the lovely 17th-century Rosenborg Castle houses the royal regalia, including the dazzling Crown Jewels *(see p16)*.

4 Latin Quarter

One of the oldest areas in Copenhagen, the Latin Quarter is just off the main pedestrianized street, Strøget *(see pp18–19)*.

5 Kongens Nytorv and Nyhavn

Kongens Nytorv (King's New Square) is a splendid Baroque square at the top of Nyhavn. Previously a seedy haunt for sailors, Nyhavn has been radically transformed. It is now a waterside attraction with bars and restaurants *(see pp22–3)*.

6 Amalienborg and Frederiksstaden

Home to the royal family since 1794, this complex of palaces represents some of the best Rococo architecture in Denmark, plus fascinating displays (see pp24–5).

7 Statens Museum for Kunst

You will find a wonderful collection of Danish and European sculpture and paintings at the National Gallery. It is housed in a beautiful 19th-century building, connected by a glass bridge to a modern wing (see pp26–7).

8 Christiania

This is a wonderland of cafés, bars, music venues, art galleries and fiercely independent shops – and a must-see for anyone interested in the city's thriving counter-culture (see pp28–9).

9 Nationalmuseet

Here is a perfect example of how brilliantly the Danes design their museums. You will find fabulous ethnographic artifacts from around the world, as well as an excellent children's museum (see pp30–31).

10 Slotsholmen

This is where it all began in the 12th century. The present Neo-Baroque castle was built in 1907–28, but was never inhabited by the monarch. It is shared between the royals and Parliament (see pp32–3).

Map markers: Kastellet, Kongens Nytorv, Nyhavn, Inderhavn

0 metres 400
0 yards 400

🔟⭐ Harbour Sights

A harbour tour is a delightful way to take in the city's brilliant views and varied topography. You will be taken along the wide waters of the Inner Harbour and winding waterways of Christianshavn, then round to Slotsholmen (the island on which the original town of Havn flourished in the 12th century). Vor Frelsers Kirke, in particular, makes a spectacular sight as you look up through the rigging of sailing boats dotting the Christianshavn canal.

① The Canals
The canals that you glide along on the tour **(above)** were built in a Dutch style in 1618 at the command of Christian IV. It is because of this that Christianshavn is referred to as "Little Amsterdam".

② Operaen
The Opera House **(below)** was built in just four years. Its massive, orange-maple coloured auditorium seats 1,700 people *(see pp94–5)*. The foyer's sculptures change colour with the weather.

③ Vor Frelsers Kirke
With a soaring twisted spire, this opulent church dominates the Christianshavn skyline. An ascent offers an unparalleled vantage point over the city.

④ Nyhavn
Even today, the utterly charming old harbour of Nyhavn is filled with boats. The old brothels and pubs have now been turned into respectable bars and restaurants serving good, traditional Danish dishes.

⑤ Den Sorte Diamant
The Black Diamond, a vast, eye-catching structure, holds all the books ever published in Denmark *(see p64)*. It is the largest library in the Nordic countries, and a great place to find original Danish texts.

7 Havnebadet

Take a refreshing dip in the sparkling clean harbour waters of this popular open-air pool **(left)**, while enjoying superb views of the city. There are three pools to choose from – for adults, for children and a smaller pool for divers *(see p49)*.

8 Langelinie

One of the city's most scenic areas, this is a wonderful place to walk along the harbour banks. Stroll along, past Kastellet and the Little Mermaid, right up to the final stretch where there is a cruise ship terminal.

MUTANT MERMAID

Set close to the Little Mermaid, and almost inviting controversy, is a sculpture group called *Paradise Genetically Altered* by Danish artist Bjørn Nørgaard. There is a triumphal arch, with a 9-m (29-ft) genetically altered Madonna atop it, surrounded by figures of Adam, Eve, Christ, Mary Magdalene, the Tripartite Capital – a critical representation of capitalism – and a pregnant man. On its own small island not far away sits the *Genetically Modified Little Mermaid*.

9 The Little Mermaid

Den Lille Havfrue is a surprisingly small landmark, ordered by brewery magnate Carl Jacobsen in 1909. It was created in 1913 *(see p80)* by Edvard Eriksen, whose wife, Eline, was the model.

10 Pavilions and the Royal Yacht

On the quayside, just beyond the Little Mermaid, are two green-domed pavilions. It is here that the Danish royal family gathers before boarding their stunning 79-m (259-ft) royal yacht, called the *Dannebrog* **(right)**, which shares its name with the Danish flag (said to have fallen from the sky in the year 1219).

6 Houseboats

The houseboats along the canals range from boat-like structures to some with barge-like designs, and other homes built on floating platforms, complete with outdoor spaces.

NEED TO KNOW
MAP L4

Stromma: 32 96 30 00; tours run daily year-round, several departures per day, check website for times; adm; www.stromma.dk

Netto Boats: 32 54 41 02; tours run daily year-round, several departures per day, check website for times (English, German, Danish tours); adm; www.havn erundfart.dk/canaltours

■ Both Stromma and Netto Boats offer guided canal and harbour tours *(see p109)*. Public buses whose routes run along the harbour include the 901 and 902 from Den Sorte Diamant, Nyhavn, Knippelsbro, Operaen, Nyholm or Larsen Plads. Buses 991, 992 and 993 run between Refshaleøen (Holmen) and Langelinie. Copenhagen Cards are also accepted *(see p112)*.

Tivoli

Famous for its magical fairy-tale ambience, exotic buildings, gorgeous landscaped gardens and upmarket entertainment and restaurants, Tivoli Gardens is more than an amusement park. The atmosphere is magical enough to merit a visit even if you are not interested in the excellent rides on offer. Founded in 1843, Tivoli has long been a favourite with royalty. It also proved to be a great source of inspiration for Walt Disney, who visited in the 1950s and is said to have been fascinated by Tivoli's atmosphere.

2 Thrill Rides
Day or night, Tivoli rings with the shrieks of people whizzing along on thrill rides such as *Aquila*, *The Demon* **(left)**, *Vertigo* and *The Starflyer*, which reaches a height of 80 m (262 ft).

1 Gentle Rides
For children and the faint-hearted, there are plenty of fun, gentle rides. The Ferris wheel is an observation wheel that offers great views over Tivoli. You could also enjoy a trolley-bus ride, a carousel ride with exotic animals and music, a waltzer in the shape of a pirate ship and several charming kids' rides, such as flying dragons and miniature classic cars.

3 Tivoli Concert Hall and Open-Air Stage
The hall hosts varied performances. There is music daily in the Harmony Pavilion, and free rock concerts on Friday nights.

4 Pantomime Theatre
Built in 1874, this theatre **(below)** has an exotic Chinese design and a spectacular stage curtain styled like a peacock's tail. It is known for its very enjoyable mime shows.

5 Dragon Boats
These boats **(above)** are very popular rides at Tivoli. Kids love floating on the lake during the day. In the evenings, the setting turns romantic.

6 Tivoli at Night
At night Tivoli is utterly magical, sparkling resplendently with thousands of fairy lights and Chinese lanterns. You can catch the dazzling Tivoli Illuminations over the lake, an exuberant, late-night show with fireworks, lasers, music and waterjets.

7 Traditional Rides

Tivoli's current Ferris wheel dates from 1943. The Roller Coaster **(left)** was built in 1914 and is one of the oldest of its kind. It reaches speeds of 58 kmph (36 mph). The classic carousel is also very popular, perfect for adults looking for a dose of nostalgia.

> **CHRISTMAS AT TIVOLI**
>
> For six weeks between mid-November and the end of December Tivoli transforms into a winter wonderland: an exciting, no-holds-barred, Father Christmas-strewn, elf driven, illuminated extravaganza that you and the kids aren't likely to forget in a hurry!

8 Tivoli Akvarium

Don't miss the amazing aquarium in the foyer of the Concert Hall. Based on a tropical coral reef, this extensive salt-water aquarium is home to more than 1,600 fish of over 500 varieties. Among the popular attractions are the eels.

9 Tivoli Youth Guard

A tradition since 1844, the Youth Guard parades through Tivoli – complete with instruments, coach and horses – forming a delightful picture.

NEED TO KNOW

MAP H5 ■

Vesterbrogade 3 ■ 33 15 10 01 ■ www.tivoli.dk

Open summer: 11am–11pm Sun–Thu, 11am–midnight Fri & Sat; winter: 11am–9pm Sun–Thu, 11am–10pm Fri & Sat (hours can vary, check website before visiting)

Adm varies (check website for details)

■ Go on the thrill rides during the day, as long queues can build up in the evenings.

10 Nimb Hotel

This splendid hotel **(below)**, housed in the Nimb building, offers a variety of culinary experiences, such as a *vinoteque*, the Andersen Bakery, a Bar'n'Grill with primed steaks and a brasserie.

TOP 10 ⭐ Rosenborg Slot and Kongens Have

Rosenborg Castle was originally built as a summer house in 1606–34 by Christian IV. At that time, it stood surrounded by sprawling gardens (now the Kongens Have park) out in the tranquil countryside. This was Christian IV's favourite castle, and many rooms retain the original Renaissance decor from his residency. When he was on his deathbed at Frederiksborg Castle in 1648, he insisted on being brought to Rosenborg Castle, and eventually died here.

① Knight's Hall
Known as the Long Hall before 1750, this room was completed in 1624 as a celebration hall. Only two Dutch fireplaces still remain from the room's original elaborate decorations.

③ Marble Hall
Originally the bedroom of Kirsten Munk, Christian IV's morganatic wife, this room (above) was turned into a Baroque show of splendour to celebrate the Absolute Monarchy.

② Royal Residence
Complete with fairy-tale turrets and bronze lions guarding the entrance (below), the castle is wholly regal. In 1838, it became the first royal residence to open to the public.

④ Crown Jewels
The castle has been used as the treasury of the realm since 1658. In the castle's heavily guarded basement are Denmark's Crown Jewels (above).

⑤ Dark Room
This room is filled with fascinating objects, such as wax portraits of Frederik III and a 17th-century trick chair.

ROSENBORG'S KINGS

Christian IV: Built many Renaissance buildings.
Frederik III: Introduced Absolute Monarchy to control the aristocracy.
Christian V: Introduced fair taxation.
Frederik IV: Constructed Frederiksberg Castle.
Christian VI: Known as the religious king.
Frederik V: Responsible for the building of the Frederiksstaden district.

⑧ Frederik IV's Chamber Room

In the 1700s, this room (above) was used by Frederik IV's sister as an antechamber and the tapestries that hang here date back to this period. Note the intricate equestrian statue of Frederik, made from silver. The coffered ceiling is the original.

⑨ Christian IV's Bedroom

Another private royal apartment, this room contains Christian IV's bloodied clothing, from the naval battle of Kolberger Heide (1644) where he lost an eye. The king wanted these clothes preserved as national mementos.

⑩ Winter Room

This panelled room (below) is said to have been one of Christian IV's most important private chambers. Look out for the speaking tubes that connect with the wine cellar and room above.

⑥ Glass Cabinet

This room was designed as a glass cabinet in 1713–14 by Frederik IV. The cabinet was built to house the extensive collection of glassware presented to Frederik in 1709 by the city of Venice, and the contents are amazing.

⑦ Kongens Have

Visited by over 2 million people every year, these are Denmark's oldest royal gardens and date back to the 17th century. There is a rose garden, which contains many statues. Various art events and a puppet theatre for children are held during summer.

NEED TO KNOW

MAP J2 ▪ Øster Voldgade 4A ▪ 33 15 32 86 ▪ www.rosenborgslot.dk

Open May, Sep & Oct: 10am–4pm daily; Jun–Aug: 9am–6pm daily; Nov–Apr: 10am–2pm Tue–Sun

Adm 110 Dkr, students 60 Dkr, senior citizens 55 Dkr, under-18s free; Kongens Have free; Copenhagen Card accepted

Guided tours (each 60–90 minutes long) are available in English, German and French (advance booking is required)

▪ Avoid lurking near the guards at the entrance to the Crown Jewels – you might be considered a security risk.

▪ There is a restaurant and a small café in Kongens Have.

TOP 10 ⭐ Latin Quarter

The Latin Quarter is home to Copenhagen's university, where Latin used to be the spoken language. One of the oldest areas in the city, it is full of 17th-century buildings that were built by the architect king, Christian IV. Although there have been dwellings here since medieval times, most of them were destroyed in the disastrous fire that spread across Copenhagen in 1728. Today, the Latin Quarter is a lively and bustling student area brimming with shops and cafés.

Højbro Plads ①
The 1902 bronze equestrian statue **(right)** on this popular square depicts the 12th-century Bishop Absalon, founder of Copenhagen, facing the site of his original castle on Slotsholmen.

② Sankt Petri Kirke
Older than Vor Frue Kirke, Copenhagen's German church also suffered from city fires and the British bombardment of 1807. Its vaulted sepulchral chapel has monuments and tombs dating back to 1681.

Latin Quarter

⑤ Rundetårn
The Round Tower was built in 1642 by Christian IV as an observatory, its official role until 1861. It is 34.8 m (114 ft) high, with an internal ramp that spirals almost to the top. It holds art exhibitions and concerts in the library (see p46).

③ Regensen
This 17th-century student residence lies opposite the Rundetårn. A part of it burned down in the great fire of 1728, but was soon rebuilt. Its students retain the old tradition of "storming" Rundetårn every May.

④ Gråbrødretorv
Named after the Grey Brothers who built Copenhagen's first monastery here, this lovely 13th-century square **(right)** is now a popular place for locals and visitors to enjoy alfresco meals or drinks.

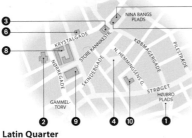

7 Trinitatis Kirke

This magnificent church **(left)** was built in 1637–56 for the staff and students of the university. If it happens to be closed when you visit, you can enter Rundetårn and get a view of the church nave through the glass panel at the start of the ramp.

8 Universitetet

Founded in 1479 by Christian I, the University of Copenhagen was the country's first university. The Neo-Classical building that can be seen here today dates to the 19th century. In the courtyard, there are the remains of an old Bishop's Palace (1420). Most of the university is now on the island of Amager.

THE BELLS AND CARILLON OF HELLIGÅNDSKIRKEN

In 1647, 50 years after the clock tower was built, king Christian IV gifted the church a set of bells and a carillon. The carillon consisted of 19 bells. It was also used at funerals; the importance of the deceased decided for how long the bells would chime – sometimes hours.

9 Vor Frue Kirke

In the 12th century, Bishop Absalon founded a Gothic church on this site. After burning down twice, the present Neo-Classical cathedral **(below)** was completed in 1829, but the tower is from medieval times.

6 Synagogen

Built from 1830–33, Copenhagen's oldest synagogue survived Nazi occupation. The synagogue for the city's Jewish community, it is not open to visitors except with prior booking.

10 Helligåndskirken

The Church of the Holy Ghost was built in 1295 as a hospital for the weak and elderly, and was expanded to include a monastery in 1474.

NEED TO KNOW

MAP J4

Synagogen: Krystalgade 12; 33 12 88 68

Rundetårn: Købmagergade 52A; 33 73 03 73; open May–Sep: 10am–8pm daily, Oct–Apr: 10am–6pm Mon, Thu–Sun, 10am–9pm Tue–Wed; adm 25 Dkr (free with Copenhagen Card); www.rundetaarn.dk

Trinitatis Kirke: Købmagergade 52A; open 9:30am–4:30pm Mon–Sat; www.trinitatis kirke.dk

Universitetet: Nørregade 10; 35 32 26 26; open 9am–5pm Mon–Fri; www.ku.dk

Vor Frue Kirke: Nørregade 8; open 8am–5pm Mon–Sat

Sankt Petri Kirke: Skt Peders St 2; 33 13 38 33; open Apr–Sep: 11am–3pm Tue–Sat; adm to the sepulchral chapel

Hellingåndskirken: Niels Hemmingsens Gade 5; 33 15 41 44; open noon–4pm Mon–Fri (7pm–midnight Fri)

Following pages Statue of Frederik V and Marmorkirken, Amalienborg

TOP 10 ⭐ Kongens Nytorv and Nyhavn

Kongens Nytorv (King's New Square) and Nyhavn (New Harbour) are two of the most picturesque areas in Copenhagen, although ongoing construction work around Kongens Nytorv has at times marred the view. The square was once outside the city gates and the site of the town gallows in medieval times. The Nyhavn canal was planned by Frederik III to connect the Inner Harbour with the square, enabling merchants to unload their goods.

1 Nyhavn Nos 18, 20 and 67

These brightly painted merchants' houses were built at the same time as the harbour. Fairy-tale writer Hans Christian Andersen lived in them – he wrote his first tale, *The Tinder Box* (1835), while living at No 20 *(see p47)*.

3 Nyhavn Canal

Running down to the Inner Harbour, this canal **(right)** is flanked by houses that belonged to merchants. A large anchor, installed in honour of the sailors who lost their lives in World War II, marks the starting point of Nyhavn.

Kongens Nytorv and Nyhavn

2 Charlottenborg Slot

An early example of the Danish Baroque style, this palace was built by Frederik III's son Ulrik. It houses the Royal Danish Academy of Fine Arts as well as the Kunsthal Charlottenborg.

4 Hotel d'Angleterre

This is Copenhagen's oldest hotel **(below)**, and one of the oldest in the world *(see p114)*. It has hosted royalty and celebrities, including Karen Blixen, Churchill, Grace Kelly and Madonna.

5 Magasin du Nord

Originally the famous Hotel du Nord, this is Copenhagen's oldest department store and is considered to be the city's answer to London's Selfridges or New York's Bloomingdale's.

6 Amber Museum

Set in a house dating back to 1606, this small museum displays an exquisite collection dedicated to Denmark's national gem, amber (also called Nordic Gold).

8 Equestrian Statue

The bronze statue in the middle of Kongens Nytorv commemorates Christian V (1646–99), who rebuilt the square in 1670 in Baroque style. Created by the French-born court sculptor Abraham-César Lamoureux, it shows the king dressed as a Roman emperor **(left)**.

"THE IMPERIAL ETHIOPIAN PALACE"

In the 1950s, Ethopia's emperor Haile Selassie, with his wife, family and entire entourage, visited Denmark and stayed at the Hotel d'Angleterre. During their stay, all telephone calls to the hotel were answered with "The Imperial Ethiopian Palace".

9 Store Strandstræde and Lille Strandstræde

Once full of pubs and brothels, "Big Beach Street" and "Little Beach Street" are now home to art galleries and stylish designer shops.

10 Det Kongelige Teater

This Baroque-style theatre is home to the Royal Danish Ballet **(below)** and is the third one to stand on this site.

7 Vingårdsstræde 6

At the age of 22, Hans Christian Andersen lived for a year in the attic of this building *(see p46)*, one of the city's oldest, built on the site of a vineyard (hence *Vingårdsstræde*). Its 13th-century cellars now host the Michelin-starred Kong Hans Kælder.

NEED TO KNOW

MAP K4–L4

Amber Museum: Kongens Nytorv 2; 33 11 67 00; open May–Sep: 10am–6:30pm daily, Oct–Apr: 10am–5:30pm daily; adm 25 Dkr, concessions 10 Dkr; www.houseofamber.com

Charlottenborg Slot: Nyhavn 2; 33 13 40 22; open 11am–5pm Tue–Sun (until 8pm Wed); adm 60 Dkr, concessions 40 Dkr, free with Copenhagen Card; www.kunsthal charlottenborg.dk

Magasin du Nord: Kongens Nytorv 13; open 10am–8pm daily; www.magasin.dk

Det Kongelige Teater: Kongens Nytorv; 33 69 69 33; guided tours available, book at the box office or in advance; www.kglteater.dk

■ The restaurants on the south side of Nyhavn are good and usually not as busy as those on the north.

■ Find a quick bite away from the crowds in Nyhavn Pizzeria at 8 Lille Strandstræde.

▣10 ★ Amalienborg and Frederiksstaden

Built in the 1750s, this stately complex was designed by the royal architect, Nicolai Eigtved. Four Rococo palaces, originally home to four noble families, enclose an octagonal square in Frederiksstaden, an aristocratic area built by Frederik V. Christian VII bought the palaces after the Christiansborg Slot burned down in 1794. The royal family has lived here ever since. It was named after a palace built on this site by Queen Sophie Amalie in the 17th century.

Christian VII's Palace ①

This palace **(right)** was one of the first to be completed by the time of Eigtved's death in 1754. Also known as Moltke Palace – named after its original owner, Count Adam Gottlob Moltke – it is the most expensive palace in the complex and also boasts one of the best Rococo interiors in the entire country.

③ Frederik VIII's Palace

This palace, with a clock on its façade, was renamed after Frederik VIII moved in. It is now the residence of Crown Prince Frederik and Crown Princess Mary.

⑤ The Golden Axis

Marmorkirken and Frederiksstaden lie on a short axis called the Golden Axis, which was considered very important when the Opera House was built.

④ Amaliehaven

The Amalie Garden was created in 1983 on the banks of the Harbour, financed by the shipping giant A P Møller and the Christine McKinney Møller Foundation. It has a splendid fountain.

② Palace Guards

When the queen is in residence, the Danish Royal Life Guards **(above)** stand outside the palace, guarding their monarch in two-hour shifts. At noon they are replaced by the guards from Rosenborg Slot, who march through the streets of Copenhagen every day just before noon.

NEED TO KNOW

MAP L3

Marmorkirken: Frederiksgade 4; 33 15 01 44; open 10am–7pm Mon–Thu, noon–5pm Fri–Sun (tower open mid-Jun–Aug: 1–3pm daily, Sep–mid-Jun: 1–3pm Sat & Sun); adm; www.marmorkirken.dk

Amalienborg Museum: 33 12 21 86; open May–Oct: 10am–4pm daily, Nov–Apr: 11am–4pm Tue–Sun; adm 70 Dkr (90 Dkr on Sat), students 50 Dkr (60 Dkr on Sat), free with Copenhagen Card; www.dkks.dk

■ Note that two palaces are closed to the public: Frederik VIII's and Christian IX's.

■ The guards will not respond well to people sitting on palace steps.

7 Colonnade

Christian VII's royal architect, Caspar Harsdorff, built this Classical-style colonnade in 1794–5. Supported by eight ionic columns, it connects two palaces.

8 Christian IX's Palace

The first royal family to live here was Crown Prince Frederik VI and his wife (1794). Since 1967, it has been home to Queen Margrethe and Prince Consort Henrik.

6 Marmorkirken

Properly called Frederikskirken, the Marble Church **(above)** got its name on account of plans to build it using Norwegian marble. Its dome, one of the largest in Europe, has a diameter of 31 m (102 ft).

Amalienborg and Frederiksstaden

9 Christian VIII's Palace

This is where Crown Prince Frederik lived until his marriage to Australian Mary Donaldson. Part of the palace is open all year round as the Amalienborg Museum **(above)**.

10 Equestrian Statue of Frederik V

Designed and cast (1753–71) by French sculptor Jacques Saly, this statue of Frederik V **(right)** is said to have cost four times as much as Amalienborg itself.

TOP 10 ⭐ Statens Museum for Kunst

The National Gallery is housed in two buildings, one from the 19th century and the other a stylish, modern extension, linked by a bridge over Sculpture Street. The museum holds international and national paintings, sculptures, prints, drawings and installations from the 14th century to the present, with the national collection specializing in Golden Age and 19th-century paintings.

① The Meeting of Joachim and Anne outside the Golden Gate of Jerusalem

Filippino Lippi (1457–1504) was a true Renaissance artist. This is evident in the architectural detail of the Corinthian columns and his paintings **(above)**.

② The Wheel of Life

Belonging to the *Suite of Seasons* series, this painting (1953) by Asger Jorn *(see p45)* represents the month of January. Jorn, who was suffering from tuberculosis, was inspired to paint this in the hope of better health.

③ The X-Room

This space has changing installations by young international artists. The black box interior is transformed into multimedia worlds.

④ Please, Keep Quiet!

Visitors have to enter this installation by Elmgreen and Dragset (2003) through swing doors, which open to a hospital ward scene. This represents the neutrality of an exhibition space.

⑤ Sculpture Street

An impressive, varied collection of sculptures by international contemporary artists runs the length of the building under a glass roof.

⑥ Christ as the Suffering Redeemer

This striking painting (1495–1500) on the traditional pietà theme by prominent Renaissance artist Andrea Mantegna shows the Resurrection of Christ on the third day after his crucifixion. Mantegna is known for his profound interest in ancient Roman civilization; in this painting it comes through in the porphyry sarcophagus.

⑦ Alice

One of over 300 portraits by Amedeo Modigliani painted between 1915 and 1920, this beautiful painting, with simple, stylized features, reflects the artist's interest in African sculpture **(below)**.

8 Romantic Paintings

Per Kirkeby is one of Denmark's most important living artists. This early collage from 1965 uses clippings from popular magazines and comics as a homage to Pop Art.

Key to Floorplan
- Ground floor
- First floor
- Second floor

The Wheel of Life **2**

Artemis **9**

The X-Room **3**

Sculpture Street **5**

Please, Keep Quiet! **4**

Portrait of Madame Matisse **10**

Alice **7**

Romantic Paintings **8**

The Meeting of Joachim and Anne outside the Golden Gate of Jerusalem **1**

Christ as the Suffering Redeemer **6**

Statens Museum for Kunst Floorplan

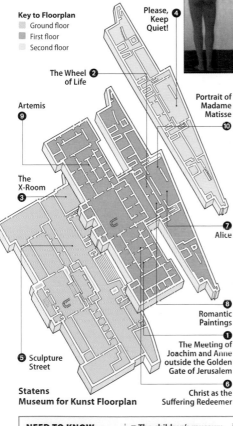

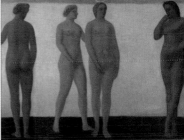

9 Artemis

Created in 1893–4, Vilhelm Hammershøi's painting (above) shows the goddess Artemis crowned with a crescent moon. The painting's Arcadian nudity, lack of depth, muted palate and enigmatic coolness are typical of Hammershøi's later work.

10 Portrait of Madame Matisse

Also known as *The Green Stripe*, this painting by Henri Matisse of his wife was to have far-reaching repercussions in the art world. It was one of several radical paintings shown in the 1905 *Salon d'Automne* and helped give rise to the Fauvist movement, known for its bright colours and spontaneous style.

NEED TO KNOW

MAP J2 ■ Sølvgade 48–50 ■ www.smk.dk

Open 11am–5pm Tue–Sun (until 8pm Wed)

Adm 110 Dkr; under-30s 85 Dkr; under-18s free

Free guided tours available

■ The prints and drawings collection dates back to the 15th century.

■ The children's museum provides activities every weekend throughout the summer holidays.

■ The bright, stylish museum café looks out onto Østre Anlæg Lake. In good weather, the park is ideal for a picnic.

Museum Guide
Enter the museum from the corner of Sølvgade and Øster Voldgade. The lobby has temporary exhibitions and a bookshop. The entire ground floor is taken up by Sculpture Street, with 20th-century Danish and international art in the extension of the first and second floor. The old main building houses European art 1300–1800, Danish and Nordic art 1750–1900 and French art 1900–1930.

Christiania

A world apart from the opulent splendour of Royal Copenhagen, this self-proclaimed "freetown" sits on the edge of one of the city's most expensive neighbourhoods. It has provided a safe haven for hippies, dreamers and nonconformists since the 1970s, when a band of ideological squatters moved into the abandoned army barracks with the aim of creating a self-sustaining community, free from the shackles of the state. Today, it's a bucolic, tumbledown wonderland of cosy cafés, bars, music venues, art galleries and shops.

1 Den Grå Hal

With its graffitied entrance (above), this is the biggest music and cultural venue in Christiania. The former stables doubles up as a unique bazaar during the Christmas period, selling everything – even locally carved instruments.

2 Badehuset

Dare to go bare at this back-to-basics nudist bathhouse; the cheapest and friendliest unisex sauna in the city. For under 50 Dkr, you can try a wonderful Moroccan *rasul* (a mineral cleanser).

3 Christiania Walking Tour

To really get a feel for the area, join one of the regular walking tours of Christiania and learn more about the fascinating history of the self-styled freetown from one of its residents. Tours depart regularly.

4 Nemoland

This former fruit and vegetable market is now one of Copenhagen's most vibrant bars, offering cheap booze and eats to be enjoyed on its terrace (below). The outdoor stage hosts regular free music concerts in the summer.

5 ALIS Wonderland

What started life as a humble skate ramp has become one of the city's best skateparks. The vibrant graffiti murals **(above)** adorning the walls are now an attraction in themselves.

8 Café Månefiskeren

This cosy café with a laid-back vibe is the perfect spot to unwind or enjoy a game of bar billiards. There's regular free jazz and reggae concerts in the quaint cobblestone courtyard.

CASTLE ISLAND

In 2004, as residents of Christiania sought to gain permanent rights from the government to occupy the area, they tried to appease the state by tearing down the colourful hash stalls that brazenly lined Pusher Street at the time. One such booth, the interestingly named "Smoke-away" stall, survived intact and has been displayed in the city's Nationalmuseet.

10 Loppen

This intimate live music venue **(below)** is a cornerstone of the city's alternative music scene. With gigs almost every night of the week, and a great programme that includes everything from Scandinavian punk to Danish dub-reggae, it's the ideal place to end your night out.

Christiania

6 Morgenstedet

Tuck into hearty vegetarian fare at this cosy cottage-style restaurant set just off Christiania's main drag. It was established over 20 years ago as a volunteer-run collective.

9 Christiania Smedie

Christiania's oldest business, this blacksmith started out producing furnaces in the early 1970s before switching its attention to building cargo bikes.

7 Galloperiet

Christiania's tongue-in-cheek tribute to the Statens Museum for Kunst (SMK), this quirky gallery houses a collection of wonderful arts and crafts.

NEED TO KNOW

MAP M5 ■ Prinsessegade, ■ www.christiania.org

■ Christiania is a car-free community, so it is best not to travel there on four wheels. On-street parking outside the pedestrianized zone is limited, so hop on a bike, or take the 9A bus from the Central Station.

■ Visitors are advised not to film or photograph in Christiania.

■ The possession and sale of cannabis are still illegal in Denmark. While police rarely venture into Christiania itself, officers regularly conduct stop-checks on people leaving the commune.

🔟⭐ **Nationalmuseet**

Denmark's largest museum, the National Museum presents the history and culture of the Danes from prehistoric times to the present. It also houses a wonderful collection of Greek and Egyptian antiquities, an ethnographic collection and the Children's Museum. Many of the displays derive from King Frederik III's Royal Cabinet of Curiosities, put together around 1650.

NEED TO KNOW

MAP J5 ■ Ny Vestergade 10 ■ 33 13 44 11 ■ www.natmus.dk

Open 10am–5pm daily

Free guided tours: Jun–Sep: 11am Tue, Thu & Sun; Oct–May: Sat & Sun

Victorian Home: Frederiksholms Kanal 18; open: Jun–Sep: 2pm Sat (only via a guided tour, buy tickets at the museum); adm 50 Dkr, concessions 40 Dkr, under-18s free

■ The Victorian Home, a plush apartment with beautiful, authentic 19th-century interiors, owned by the museum, is located nearby.

■ Have brunch or open sandwiches at the café.

Museum Guide

Fronted by a courtyard, the museum's entrance hall has toilets, lockers and the museum shop, which sells interesting books and educational toys with a Viking twist. The Children's Museum *(see p52)* is to your left. The ground floor has the prehistoric collection, while the first floor has a range of displays. There's a Danish history collection on the second floor, and the antiquities are on the third floor. Temporary exhibitions rotate regularly.

1 Room 117

This 18th-century bourgeois interior can be traced to the town of Aalborg in Jutland. A room in a sea of glass-display galleries, it features a heavy wooden four-poster bed **(above)**, chest, coffered wooden ceiling and mullioned windows.

2 Denmark's Oldest Coin

The name of Denmark and an image of a Danish king are depicted on this silver coin, displayed in Room 144, that was struck in AD 995.

5 Gundestrup Cauldron

Found near Gundestrup, this lovely silver cauldron from the Iron Age is decorated with animals and mystical figures.

3 Prehistoric Denmark and the Viking Age

The museum's most popular exhibit is this display of the country's 14,000-year history. These intricate golden horns **(right)** were reconstructed in the 20th century.

4 Cylinder Perspective Table

Part of Frederik III's Royal Cabinet of Curiosities, the table shows him and his wife painted ingeniously in a distorted perspective, rectified when viewed in the reflective cylinder.

Sun Chariot ⑥

The unique Sun Chariot or Solvognen **(right)** was dug up in 1902 by a farmer who was ploughing his field. This 3,400-year-old artifact from the Bronze Age shows a wheeled horse pulling a large sun disk gilded on one side.

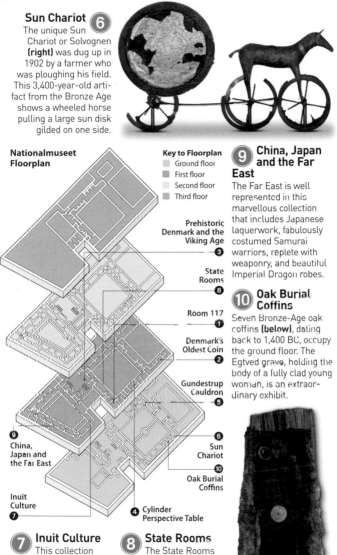

Nationalmuseet Floorplan

Key to Floorplan
- Ground floor
- First floor
- Second floor
- Third floor

Prehistoric Denmark and the Viking Age ❸

State Rooms ❽

Room 117 ❶

Denmark's Oldest Coin ❷

Gundestrup Cauldron ❺

❻ Sun Chariot

❿ Oak Burial Coffins

❹ Cylinder Perspective Table

❾ China, Japan and the Far East

❼ Inuit Culture

⑨ China, Japan and the Far East

The Far East is well represented in this marvellous collection that includes Japanese laquerwork, fabulously costumed Samurai warriors, replete with weaponry, and beautiful Imperial Dragon robes.

⑩ Oak Burial Coffins

Seven Bronze-Age oak coffins **(below)**, dating back to 1,400 BC, occupy the ground floor. The Egtved grave, holding the body of a fully clad young woman, is an extraordinary exhibit.

⑦ Inuit Culture

This collection from Greenland showcases the skill and creative ingenuity of the people of the frozen North. The displays include clothing, such as embroidered anoraks and boots, plus toys and watercolours of daily life.

⑧ State Rooms

The State Rooms date back to the time when this building was a royal palace. They have been well preserved and are virtually intact from the period 1743–4. Next-door, the Great Hall is adorned with the original Flemish tapestries.

TOP 10 ⭐ Slotsholmen

The small fishing village of Copenhagen was founded on the island of Slotsholmen in the 12th century. Bishop Absalon, the king's friend, built a castle here in 1167. Two centuries later, the castle was destroyed by the Hanseatic League, the European trade alliance, which resented Copenhagen's increasing control over trade. Christiansborg Slot, which stands here today, is home to the Danish Parliament, the Jewish Museum and the Palace Church.

1 Christianborg Tårnet

At 106 m (348 ft), the tower of Christiansborg Slot is the highest in Copenhagen and offers a magnificent panoramic view of the city. It is free to enter (closed Monday), but be sure to reserve in advance if you want to eat in the tower's upscale Nordic restaurant.

2 Christiansborg Slotskirke

On the site of the original 18th-century church destroyed in the ferocious palace fire of 1794, this Neo-Classical church was built in 1813–26 (see p39). However, a fire broke out in 1992 and destroyed its roof, dome and even parts of the interior. A service is held here in October to mark the opening of Parliament.

4 Tøjhusmuseet

Built as an arsenal in 1604–8, the Royal Danish Arsenal Museum is filled with artillery guns. The Armoury Hall has 7,000 hand weapons, some from the 1300s.

5 Christiansborg Slot

Designed in a Neo-Baroque style in 1907–28, this palace houses the Folketinget (the Parliament), the Prime Minister's apartment, the High Court and the State Rooms (above) used by the royal family for functions – note the marble- and silk-adorned Throne Room and Great Hall.

3 Thorvaldsens Museum

This museum is home to almost all of the works and some of the personal belongings of Danish sculptor Bertel Thorvaldsen (see p45). In the entrance hall (below) are the original plaster casts of his most famous pieces.

6 Teatermuseet

This delightful court theatre, above the Royal Stables, was established in 1767. Now a museum (see p44), it depicts Danish theatre in the 18th and 19th centuries. Visitors can also walk onto the stage.

The Top 10 of Everything

Marble sculptures at the Ny Carlsberg Glyptotek museum

8 Dansk Jødisk Museum

This museum has a striking, modern interior **(left)**, designed by Polish-American architect Daniel Libeskind. The building brilliantly depicts the lives and culture of the Jewish population in Denmark *(see p44)*.

9 Ruins Under the Palace

These fascinating ruins were discovered during the construction of the present palace. Notable are parts of Bishop Absalon's castle, the second castle that stood here until the 18th century, and details of the routine of daily life.

> **CASTLE ISLAND**
>
> Several castles have stood on this island through the centuries. The first one was built in 1167 by Bishop Absalon. A second castle, used by King Erik of Pomerania, was built in 1416. When the building started to fall apart, it was pulled down and demolished in 1731 by Christian VI. In its place, he built a palace suitable for an Absolute Monarch. It was completed in 1740, but was destroyed in the fire of 1794. Another castle, built in 1803–28, burned down in 1884. The present castle was built in 1907–28.

10 Royal Library Gardens

Formerly a naval port, this attractive oasis is tucked away behind Christiansborg **(below)**. Designed in 1920, the fountains in the central pool cascade every hour *(see p51)*. Do not overlook the statue of philosopher Søren Kierkegaard.

7 Royal Stables

The stables of Christian VI's Palace survived the fire of 1794. The Queen's horses are still kept here amid splendid marble walls, columns and mangers. There is also a collection of royal coaches and riding gear.

NEED TO KNOW
MAP J5

Christiansborg Slot: 33 92 64 92; open May–Sep: 10am–5pm daily, Oct–Apr: 10am–5pm Tue–Sun; tours of State Rooms May–Sep: 3pm daily, Oct–Apr: 3pm Tue–Sun; adm 90 Dkr, under-18s free; www.christiansborg.dk

Ruins Under the Palace: open May–Sep: 10am–5pm daily, Oct–Apr: 10am–5pm Tue–Sun; adm 50 Dkr, under-18s free

Royal Stables: open May–Sep: 1:30–4pm daily, Oct–Apr: 1:30–4pm Tue–Sun; adm 50 Dkr, under-18s free

Royal Library Gardens: 6am–10pm daily

Christiansborg Slotskirke: open 10am–5pm daily

Tøjhusmuseet: 33 11 60 37; open noon–4pm Tue–Sun

Thorvaldsens Museum: Bertel Thorvaldsens Plads 2; 33 32 15 32; open 10am–5pm Tue–Sun; adm 70 Dkr (free Wed), under-18s free; www.thorvaldsensmuseum.dk

The Top 10 of Everything

Marble sculptures at the Ny
Carlsberg Glyptotek museum

Moments in History

1 c.1000: Bishop Absalon's Castle

Copenhagen was founded around AD 1000 on Slotsholmen *(see p32)* and prospered greatly from the shoals of herring that appeared in its waters. In the 1160s Havn was given by Valdemar I to his adviser, Bishop Absalon, who built a castle as protection against raiders. The prosperity of Havn became a threat to the Hanseatic League. They attacked the castle, destroying it in 1369.

Statue of Bishop Absalon

2 1416: Copenhagen, Capital of Denmark

King Erik VII (also called Erik of Pomerania) took up residence in the second castle in 1416, by which time Havn was a major economic centre. It was proclaimed the capital of Denmark in 1443.

3 1479: The Founding of the University of Copenhagen

King Christian I inaugurated the University of Copenhagen on 1 June 1479. It had four faculties – Theology, Law, Medicine and Philosophy – and like others of the time was part of the Roman Catholic Church. It was re-established in 1537 by Christian III after the Reformation.

4 1534–36: Civil War and Reformation

Between 1534 and 1536, the Protestant Christian III successfully withstood an uprising against him that favoured Christian II, his Catholic cousin. Christian III brought about the Reformation in Denmark.

5 1660: Absolute Monarchy

Frederik III introduced Absolute Monarchy in 1660, enhancing the powers of Copenhagen's middle classes. Frederik VII abolished it in 1848.

6 1657: Wars with Sweden

The Swedes and Danes were in dispute over the Sound. In 1657, the Swedes crossed the Sound on foot, attacking Copenhagen. The Treaty of Roskilde saw Denmark cede its Swedish territories.

Painting of Copenhagen in 1660

7 1711–12: The Great Plague

Between June 1711 and March 1712, Copenhagen was hit by bubonic plague, wiping out 20,000 of its 60,000 inhabitants. It is said to have been brought in by ships from Sweden or East Prussia, carrying infected vermin.

8 1728: The Great Fire

In October, within four days, the greatest fire in Copenhagen's history wiped out almost all of the north of the city. It began early in the morning at Vester Kvarter 146 – now roughly at the top of Strøget. Five churches, the university library and 1,600 houses were destroyed.

The Battles of Copenhagen

9 1801 and 1807: The Battles of Copenhagen

Early in the 19th century, the city suffered more lasting damage when the British attacked in 1801, destroying the Danish navy, and again in 1807 to discourage the Danes from supporting France in the Napoleonic Wars.

10 1943: Rescue of the Danish Jews

The Nazis occupied Denmark during World War II from 1940 to 1945. In 1943, when they ordered that all Danish Jews were to be deported to Germany, a collective of Danes and Swedes secretly evacuated virtually the entire Jewish population to Sweden by sea. As a result, most Danish Jews survived the war.

TOP 10 HISTORICAL FIGURES

Knud Rasmussen (1879–1933)

1 Harald Bluetooth (911–987)
King Harald converted the country of Denmark to Christianity.

2 King Cnut (994/5–1035)
Cnut ruled England, Norway and Denmark for 20 years and famously failed to hold back the waves.

3 Bishop Absalon (1128–1201)
Counsellor to King Valdemar I, he built the first castle on Slotsholmen.

4 Tycho Brahe (1546–1601)
Brahe's astronomical tables were used to plot the rules of planetary motion.

5 Christian IV (1577–1648)
Christian IV promoted shipping and overseas trade and built the Rundetårn and Rosenborg Slot.

6 Vitus Jonassen Bering (1681–1741)
A fearless Danish explorer who discovered the Bering Strait, Sea, Island and Land Bridge.

7 Hans Christian Ørsted (1777–1851)
Danish physicist and chemist who discovered electromagnetism.

8 Søren Kierkegaard (1813–55)
A Danish philosopher who first put forward the theory of "existentialism".

9 Knud Rasmussen (1879–1933)
The first man to cross the Northwest Passage by dogsled.

10 Niels Bohr (1885–1962)
A Nobel Prize-winner (1922), Bohr's research contributed vastly to the understanding of quantum mechanics.

🔟 Churches

Gilded Baroque altarpiece inside Holmens Kirke

① Holmens Kirke

Built from 1562–3 as a naval forge, it was converted into a church in 1619 *(see p41)*. The Baroque altarpiece is exceptionally ornate, and the pulpit is the tallest in Denmark.

② Grundtvigs Kirke

På Bjerget 14B, Bispebjerg ▪ 35 81 54 42 ▪ **Open 9am–4pm Mon–Sat, noon–4pm Sun (Nov–Apr: until 1pm)** ▪ **www.grundtvigskirke.dk**

This parish church was built by P V Jensen Klint and his son, Kaare Klint, from 1921–6. It has yellow-brick walls and a modern Gothic appearance.

③ Trinitatis Kirke

Standing next door to the Rundetårn is the Trinitatis Kirke *(see p19)*. Commissioned by Christian IV in 1637, this lovely church was completed in the reign of Frederik III in 1656. The present interior dates back to 1731, as the original was burnt in the fire of 1728. It includes boxed pews with seashell carvings, a gilded altarpiece, a Baroque dark wood pulpit and a fabulous gold and silver organ.

④ Christians Kirke

Built in the Rococo style in 1755–9 by Nicolai Eigtved, Frederik V's master architect, Christians Kirke is starkly different from most Danish churches. Instead of the congregation sitting only in pews in the nave, the church has a second gallery level (like that of a theatre) where all the important worshippers were seated *(see p93)*.

⑤ Vor Frelsers Kirke

This splendid Baroque church was built in 1682–96 at the behest of Christian V. The king's royal insignia can be seen at various places in the church, including on the organ case,

Imposing exterior of Grundtvigs Kirke

which is supported by elephants, the symbol of Denmark's prestigious Order of the Elephant (see p43). The spire is 90 m (295 ft) high, and the tower affords a magnificent view of the city. The interior of the church is bright and well lit, thanks to the white walls and tall windows (see p94).

6 Helligåndskirken

Dating back to the 12th century, these are among the oldest architectural remains in the city of Copenhagen. Only Helligåndshuset (now used for markets and monthly exhibitions), Christian IV's Baroque portal and Griffenfeld's Chapel survive. Much of the original church burnt down in the fire of 1728. The church re-opened after reconstruction in 1732 (see p19).

7 Vor Frue Kirke

Known as St Mary's Cathedral, the church has been on this site in different forms since the 12th century and has played host to royal and national events over the years. It has a 19th-century façade and a bright interior dominated by statues of Christ and his Apostles (see p19).

8 Sankt Petri Kirke

This is the city's oldest church. Unlike most medieval buildings, it survived the fire of 1728. Its tower, nave and choir date back to the 15th

century, while the north and south transepts were added years later, in 1634 (see pp18–19).

9 Christiansborg Slotskirke

The original 18th-century Rococo creation was destroyed in the palace fire of 1794 and was rebuilt in a Neo-Classical style. Inaugurated on Whit Sunday in 1826, it succumbed to another fire in 1992, but has now been rebuilt (see pp32–3).

Ornate interior of Marmorkirken

10 Marmorkirken

This circular church, designed by Nicolai Eigtved in 1740, has an imposing presence. Work on the building was suspended in 1770 due to increasing expenses, and began again after nearly 150 years. It was eventually inaugurated on 19 August 1894 (see pp24–5).

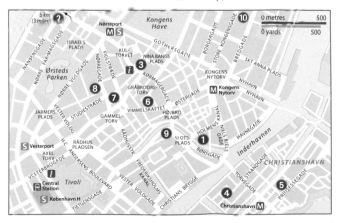

🔟 Landmark Buildings

Entrance to the Rundetårn

1 Rundetårn
This curious Round Tower was built by Christian IV and affords a wonderful view over the city's old town. It also has a popular gallery that holds innovative, changing exhibitions (see pp18–19).

2 Den Sorte Diamant
The Black Diamond (see p64) was built by architects Schmidt, Hammer and Lassen. It houses the National Museum of Photography, the Queen's Hall concert space, an exhibition area and Søren K, a smart restaurant. The shiny tiled exterior is highly reflective and a favourite photo opportunity for the boat-trippers floating past (see p12).

Frederiksborg Slot

3 Børsen
MAP K5 ▪ Børsgade ▪ Not open to the public
The stock exchange is remarkable for its tower with a striking spire design. The three crowns at the top of the building represent Denmark, Sweden and Norway.

4 Rosenborg Slot
This lovely, turreted Renaissance castle was built by Christian IV. Now a royal museum, its collections and interior provide a vivid picture of the monarchy over the centuries. The crown jewels are in the basement (see pp16–17).

5 Regensen
Built by Christian IV in the 17th century as a student hostel, Regensen still retains that function today (see p18). Unfortunately, most of the original building was burnt down in the city fire of 1728, but it was rebuilt shortly after.

6 Christiansborg Slot
This Neo-Baroque palace, built in the early 20th century, is the seat of the government and the fifth palace to have been built on the site. Visit the ruins of the first two castles, the theatre and stables and the State Rooms (see pp32–3).

7 Frederiksborg Slot
This beautiful, grand Renaissance castle is a short train ride out of Copenhagen. Christian IV was living here when he fell ill and demanded to be taken to Rosenborg, for his last few days. Don't miss the castle's ornate chapel (see p100).

8 Radisson Blu Royal Hotel

Designed by Danish architect Arne Jacobsen, this hotel (see p116) underwent a makeover in the 1980s. The original interior was retained only in Room 606; if it is unoccupied you might be able to have a look at it. The foyer has a 1960s retro look and includes Jacobsen's Swan and Egg chairs. You can enjoy views of the city from the restaurant (see p88).

9 Operaen

The Opera House auditorium is a masterpiece of acoustic design, from the velour seats that do not absorb sound to the distance from the front of the stage to the back wall, which allows for the perfect time to achieve greatest clarity. Over 100,000 pieces of 23.75 carat gold leaf make up the ceiling (see pp94–5).

Waterfront Operaen

10 Holmens Kirke

MAP K5 ■ Holmens Kanal ■ 33 13 61 78 ■ Open 10am–4pm Mon, Wed, Fri & Sat, 10am–3:30pm Tue & Thu, noon–4pm Sun

The only Renaissance church in Copenhagen was built as a sailors' forge in 1562–3 and converted into a church by Christian IV in 1619. The metal fence shows golden elephants carrying black castles on their backs, the royal Danish elephant.

TOP 10 STATUES

Carlsberg Brewery elephants

1 The Elephant Gate
MAP A6
Big, splendid elephants at the Carlsberg Brewery gate.

2 Gefionspringvandet
MAP M2
Fountain depicting the goddess Gefion as she drives an animal-led chariot and ploughs Zealand (see p80).

3 Fiskerkone
MAP J4
The *Fishwife* was created in 1940 and installed at this spot.

4 Lurblæserne
MAP H5
It is said that the *Hornblowers* will sound the Viking horns whenever a virgin passes by.

5 Frederik V
MAP L3
Sculptor Jacques Saly took 18 years to finish this statue (see p25). Unveiled in 1771, it merited a 27-gun salute.

6 Christian V
MAP J3
This shows the king dressed as a Roman emperor on horseback (see p23).

7 Hans Christian Andersen
MAP H5
Famous sculpture by Henry Lukow-Nielsen (see p72).

8 Hans Christian Andersen
MAP J2
Includes scenes from his fairy tales.

9 Caritas Springvandet
MAP H4
One of the oldest statues in Copenhagen, dating back to 1608.

10 The Little Mermaid
MAP M1
This is the city's icon, inspired by the famous fairy tale (see p80).

🔟 Sights of Royal Copenhagen

Chandeliers and artworks in the opulent hallway of Christiansborg Slot

1 Christiansborg Slot

This is the fifth castle to have been built on this site. The first, Bishop Absalon's fortified castle (1167), was destroyed in 1369. The castle built in 1740 was the first to be called Christiansborg; it was destroyed by fire in 1794. Today's castle is home to the Danish Parliament *(see pp32–3)*.

2 Fredensborg Slot

Slottet 1B, 3480 Fredensborg ■ **33 40 31 87** ■ **Open Jul 1–4:30pm daily (with guided tours); gardens: Jul 9am–5pm** ■ **Adm; free entry to gardens** ■ **Bus 173E**

This 18th-century Baroque palace is the Queen's summer home. The beautiful gardens are among Denmark's largest.

3 Kronborg Slot

This castle, built as a fortress in the 15th century, was used as a prison and army barracks until 1922 *(see p104)*. It is now occasionally used for royal functions. You may even hear a salute being fired whenever the royal yacht passes by.

4 Frederiksborg Slot

Christian IV built this Dutch Renaissance-style castle between 1602 and 1620. It is notable for its spires, copper roofs and sweeping gables. After it was destroyed in a fire in 1859, the Carlsberg Brewery magnate Jacob Jacobsen helped rebuild it. The gardens are the only royal gardens to have escaped being updated to the 19th-century Romantic style *(see p100)*.

5 Amalienborg

Two of the palaces here are open to the public; the other two are royal homes. Queen Margrethe resides in Christian IX's Palace and Crown Prince Frederik in Frederik VIII's Palace *(see pp24–5)*.

Fredensborg Slot

6 Crown Jewels

These symbols of monarchy, kept in the stronghold basement of Rosenborg Slot, include the crown, sceptre, orb, sword of state, ampulla (flask for anointing the monarch) and royal jewellery (see p16).

7 Rosenborg Slot

This delightful Renaissance palace is the oldest royal palace standing in its original form. Set in Kongens Have, it also has a delightful rose garden (see pp16–17).

8 Royal Copenhagen Porcelain

The traditional Royal Copenhagen design, "Blue Floral", dates back to the factory's initiation in 1775. The pottery features a blue design because in earlier times cobalt was the only colour able to withstand extremely high firing temperatures (see p73).

Roskilde Domkirke

9 Roskilde Domkirke

Danish royals, including Harald Bluetooth (see p37), have been buried at Roskilde since the 12th century. The cathedral houses 39 tombs, the oldest belonging to Margrethe I (d.1412) (see p102).

10 Vor Frue Kirke

St Mary's Cathedral has been a place of royal ceremony since the 13th century and was the setting for the marriage of Margrethe I to King Håkon VI of Norway in 1363. The weddings of Christian I (1449) and Crown Prince Frederik (2004) also took place here (see p19).

TOP 10 CROWN JEWELS

1 Christian IV's Crown
Made in 1595–6 by Dirich Fyring, this crown features diamonds, gold, enamel and pearls.

2 The Queen's Crown
The large, square, table-cut diamonds in Queen Sophie Magdalene's crown of 1731 are believed to have come from Queen Sophie Amalie's crown (1648).

3 Baptismal Set
Four-piece gold and silver baptismal set (1671), thought to have been first used for Crown Prince Frederik.

4 Regalia
Sceptre, orb, globe and ampulla made for Frederik III's coronation. Used at subsequent coronations until 1840.

5 Order of the Elephant
The order was founded by Christian I around 1450. The chain is made of gold, enamel, diamonds and pearls.

6 Order of the Dannebrog
Established in 1671 as part of the measures introduced by the Absolute monarchs to manage their subjects.

7 Jewellery Sets
Includes pearl set (1840) made from Charlotte Amalie's jewellery; diamond set (18th century), emerald set (1723).

8 Oldenburg Horn
This is an enamelled, silver-gilt drinking horn.

9 The King's Law 1665
Absolutism's constitution, made from parchment, silk, gold and silver.

10 Christian V's Crown
Christian V's Absolutist crown (1670–71) has a large, rare sapphire believed to be a present from the Duke of Milan to Christian I in 1474.

The stunning crown of Christian V

Museums and Galleries

The Danish Jødisk Museum

1 Dansk Jødisk Museum

MAP K5 ■ Proviant-passangen 6 ■ 33 11 22 18 ■ Open Sep–May: 1pm–4pm Tue–Fri, noon–5pm Sat–Sun; Jun–Aug: 10am–5pm Tue–Sun ■ Adm; free with Copenhagen Card ■ www.jewmus.dk

The Danish Jewish Museum tells the story of Denmark's Jewish community. Designed by architect Daniel Libeskind, the interlocking interior symbolizes Danish–Jewish good relations, its apogee the rescue of 7,000 Jews from the Nazis.

2 Designmuseum Danmark

Denmark's largest museum devoted to design, the Designmuseum holds Chinese and Japanese artifacts, along with European medieval and Rococo arts. The other half is dedicated to cutting-edge Danish 20th- and 21st-century design *(see p79)*.

The Ny Carlsberg Glyptotek

3 Teatermuseet

MAP J5 ■ Christiansborg Ridebane 18 ■ 33 11 51 76 ■ Open noon–4pm Tue–Sun ■ Adm; free with Copenhagen Card ■ www.teatermuseet.dk

On display at this enthralling museum are sections including the stage, the auditorium and dressing rooms of the 18th-century Royal Theatre *(see p46)* that survived the devastating fire of 1794.

4 Frihedsmuseet

The Museum of Danish Resistance explores Danish life during the Nazi occupation of 1940–45. The museum is currently closed until the end of 2019 due to extensive fire damage *(see p79)*.

5 Nationalmuseet

At Denmark's largest museum of cultural history you can explore the history of the Danes right up to the present day *(see pp30–31)*. Artifacts range from Iron Age burials and Renaissance interiors to African masks and houses on stilts. Check out the museum's spectacular ethno-graphic collection, including the world's oldest painting by South American Indians.

6 Ny Carlsberg Glyptotek

This museum houses a fabulous collection of antiquities from the Mediterranean coast, Egypt, Greece and Rome. You will also find an impressive collection of 19th- and 20th-century Danish and French fine art on display *(see p70)*.

7 Cisternerne – The Cisterns

Beneath the manicured lawns of Frederiksberg Have, this exhibition space is remarkable for both its provocative contemporary art and film installations and the singularity of its setting: a 19th-century cistern (see p88).

8 Davids Samling

Set inside a 19th-century town house, the museum holds the collections of Christian Ludwig David (1878–1960), a Danish barrister. It includes fabulous furniture and ancient Islamic ornamental art (see p78).

Entrance, Statens Museum for Kunst

9 Statens Museum for Kunst

Nestled in a park with lakes and grassy slopes, the National Gallery displays a collection of international art (see pp26–7), with works by Great Masters like Dürer and Titian and by icons such as Picasso and Matisse. These are displayed with 20th-century Danish works, including those of the CoBrA group.

10 Thorvaldsens Museum

Opened in 1848, this museum pays homage to the Neo-Classical sculptor Bertel Thorvaldsen (see pp32–3). It includes most of his works, as well as some private belongings. You can also visit his grave.

TOP 10 DANISH ARTISTS

Sculpture by Bertel Thorvaldsen

1 Bertel Thorvaldsen (1770–1844)
Son of an Icelandic wood carver, Thorvaldsen became Denmark's most famous sculptor.

2 Christoffer Eckersberg (1783–1853)
Laid the foundations for Denmark's Golden Age of painting (1800–50).

3 Michael Ancher (1849–1927)
One of the best-known artists in Denmark and the unofficial head of the Skagen group.

4 Peder Severin Krøyer (1851–1909)
His work is inspired by the lives of the fishermen of Skagen.

5 Anna Ancher (1859–1935)
A Skagen artist and wife of Michael Ancher. Her work is typified by picturesque scenes of family life.

6 Vilhelm Hammershøi (1864–1916)
Known for his paintings of interiors, done in muted colours.

7 Richard Mortensen (1910–1993)
The first Danish artist to turn to abstraction. Also known for his perfect technical finish.

8 Asger Jorn (1914–73)
Founder of CoBrA, an important art group to emerge after World War II.

9 Bjørn Nørgaard (1947–)
One of the most influential Danish contemporary artists, his works span a range of fields, including sculpture. He also designed the Queen's Tapestries.

10 Olafur Eliasson (1967–)
Danish–Icelandic artist who erects fascinating kinetic sculptures inspired by natural phenomena in cities around the world.

⭐️🔟 Hans Christian Andersen Sights

Hotel d'Angleterre, overlooking gardens

1 Hotel d'Angleterre

Hans Christian Andersen stayed here in November 1860, when he occupied two rooms at the corner of Kongens Nytorv and Østergade (Strøget), close to the Royal Theatre. He also stayed between August 1869 and March 1870, and, finally, during April and May 1871 *(see p114)*.

2 Det Kongelige Teater

Andersen arrived in the city on 6 September 1819 as a starstruck 14-year-old boy. It was "my second birthday", he recounts in his 1855 biography, *The Fairy Tale of My Life*. Determined to become an actor, he went straight to the Royal Theatre *(see p23)* in search of a job. Although he was occasionally employed as an actor, his acting talent never quite matched his skill as a writer.

3 Lille Kongensgade 1
MAP K4

On 23 October 1866, Andersen took a suite of rooms on the third floor here, rented to him by a photographer, Thora Hallager. It was here that he bought furniture for the first time in his life (at the age of 61), as the apartment was an unfurnished one.

4 Rundetårn

The exhibition space here was once the university library where Andersen spent many hours. His first fairy tale, *The Tinderbox* (1835), talks of a dog with eyes "as big as a tower" guarding a treasure. Scholars believe this refers to the Rundetårn, which was originally built as an observatory – a literal eye to the sky *(see pp18–19)*.

5 Vingårdsstræde 6
MAP K4

Andersen lived here (then No 132) for a year in 1827 in a spartan garret room, preparing for his university exams. This is where he wrote the poem *The Student*. Once a museum, the room is no longer open to visitors.

6 Bakkehusmuseet

The Bakkehus (House on the Hill) was the home of prominent literary patron Knud Lyne Rahbek and his wife, Kamma, from 1802 to 1830. Andersen met the couple in the early 1820s and their home soon became a meeting place for poets and authors *(see p89)*.

Bookshelves in Bakkehusmuseet

⑦ Nyhavn Nos 18, 20 and 67

Andersen lived in lodgings on and around Nyhavn for much of his life (*see p22*), including at Nyhavn 280 (now No 20) in 1834, No 67 in 1848 and No 18 (a private hotel) in 1871. He lived here until 1875, when he fell terminally ill and moved in with the Melchiors, who then nursed him in their own home.

⑧ Assistens Kirkegård

This is the cemetery where Andersen's body was interred in Nørrebro (*see p77*). The stone is inscribed with inspirational lines from his poem *Oldingen*, also known as *The Old Man* (1874).

Assistens Kirkegård

⑨ Magasin du Nord

In 1838, Andersen moved into Hotel du Nord, now the department store Magasin du Nord (*see pp22–3*). Here he proceeded to rent two rooms in the attic, one of which overlooked the Royal Theatre. The next-door Mini's Café became a regular haunt for the writer.

⑩ Vor Frue Kirke

Andersen died on 4 August 1875 of liver cancer. His funeral, a national event attended by the king and crown prince, was held at Vor Frue Kirke in the old town (*see p19*).

TOP 10 DANISH CULTURAL FIGURES

Actor Viggo Mortensen

1 August Bournonville (1805–1879)
Choreographer and ballet master who created many works.

2 Carl Nielsen (1865–1931)
Composer, violinist and pianist. Best known for his symphonies and the operas *Saul og David* and *Maskerade*.

3 Karen Blixen (1885–1962)
Her famous novel, *Out of Africa* (1937), was published under the pen name Isak Dinesen.

4 Poul Henningsen (1894–1967)
This anti-traditionalist, architect and author is best known for his PH lamps (*see p63*).

5 Arne Jacobsen (1902–1971)
Architect and designer who defined the concept of Danish design – fluid and practical.

6 Lars von Trier (1956–)
Film director famous for the Dogme95 Collective and his technique of cinematic minimalism.

7 Viggo Mortensen (1958–)
Popular as Aragorn in *The Lord of the Rings* films.

8 Mads Mikkelsen (1965–)
Made his international acting breakthrough as Bond villain Le Chiffre in *Casino Royale*.

9 Helena Christensen (1968–)
Miss Denmark (1986) and a supermodel of the 1990s.

10 Sofie Gråbøl (1968–)
Played detective Sarah Lund in hit crime series *Forbrydelsen* (*The Killing*).

🔟 Outdoor Activities

Browsing the flea market at Nørrebro

1 Flea Markets
**Frederiksberg Rådhusplads:
MAP A5; Apr–Oct: 8am–3pm Sat
■ Bertel Thorvaldsens Plads: MAP J5;
May–Sep: 8am–5pm Fri, 9am– 5pm
Sat ■ Ravnsborggade, Nørrebro: MAP
D3; Mar–Nov: 10am–4pm Sun**
There are many outdoor flea
markets in the summer, offering
everything from furniture to vinyl.

2 CopenHot
**Sankt Annæ Plads 31 ■ 31 32
78 08 ■ www.copenhot.com**
The purveyors of Copenhagen's only
floating hot-tub experience, this
open-air spa brings Nordic wellness
to the city centre. With three giant
hot tubs, a sauna with panoramic
views of the harbour and five "sailing
spa" boats, it's the perfect place to
escape the hustle and bustle of the
city. There's even speakers to play
your own music.

3 Bikes
Almost every major road in
Copenhagen has a cycle lane and
you can hire a bike or use a free City
Bike for a day or more (see p109).

Canal tour in Nyhavn

4 Go Boats
**Islands Brygge 10 ■ 40 26 10
25 ■ www.goboat.dk**
If you prefer to explore the city's
waterways at your own pace, hop
on board a solar-powered Go Boat
and spend an afternoon chugging
through the canals. You can buy a
picnic hamper or champagne to take
on board, although the captain must
always remain sober while in control
of their vessel!

5 Lounging by the Lakes
Man-made lakes divide
the main city from Nørrebro and
Østerbro. Of these, Skt Jørgens Sø,
Peblinge Sø and Sortedams Sø are
easily accessible. You can lounge
along their grassy banks or enjoy
the scenic view from the bridges.

6 Kongens Have
Attached to Rosenborg Slot,
the King's Garden is a great place to
sunbathe, play frisbee, cricket or
football, or have a picnic. In the
summer, you can catch a puppet
show or a jazz concert (see p17.

7 Canal tours
Harbour and canal tours are a
lovely way to see the city. There are
two canal tour companies (see p13).

8 Assistens Kirkegård
This beautiful, meandering churchyard holds the graves of famous Danes like Hans Christian Andersen, August Bournonville and Niels Bohr *(see p77)*.

9 Dyrehaven
MAP B2 ■ Dyrehaven, Klampenborg ■ www.bakken.dk
This deer park has been here since the 16th century and is home to over 2,000 deer (the rutting season is in the autumn). It is like an English park or common and features a noisy, enjoyable funfair, which is called Bakken *(see p52)*.

Elephants at Zoologisk Have

10 Zoologisk Have
You will find polar bears, lions, tigers, elephants and other animals in this delightful zoo *(see p88)*. There are wonderful thematic adventure trails for kids *(see p53)*.

TOP 10 BEACHES AND POOLS

Diving at Havnebadet

1 Havnebadet
Floating harbour pool with fresh water *(see p64)*.

2 Bellevue
MAP B2 ■ Strandvejen 340, 2930 Klampenborg
Full of people playing, sailing or relaxing. Left end is nudist.

3 Fælledparkens Soppesø
MAP D2 ■ Borgmester Jensens Allé 50, Østerbro ■ 33 66 36 60
Huge, child-friendly, outdoor pool.

4 Amager Strandpark
MAP B3 ■ Amager Strandvej
Luxury Beach with lagoon, artificial island and snack kiosks.

5 Køge Bugt Strandpark
MAP B3 ■ Ishøj Store Torv 20, 2635 Ishøj
A 7-km (4-mile) beach along Køge Bay.

6 Bellahøj Svømmestadion
MAP B3 ■ Bellahøjvej 1–3, Brønshøj ■ 38 26 21 40
Indoor and outdoor swimming facilities, including water slides.

7 Frederiksdal Friluftsbad
MAP B2 ■ Frederiksdal Badesti 1, Virum ■ 45 83 81 85
Gorgeous lakeside beach with café.

8 DGI-Byen
MAP D5 ■ Corner of Tietgensgade & Ingerslevsgade ■ 33 29 81 40
Indoor facilities with a kids' pool.

9 Charlottenlund Beach
MAP B2 ■ Park Strandvejen 144, Charlottenlund
Good place for sunbathing.

10 Copencabana Havnebadet ved Fisketorvet
MAP E6 ■ Havneholmen 0, Vesterbro ■ 27 52 90 28
A floating harbour pool.

TOP 10 Off the Beaten Track

Crowds wait outside Mikkeller

① **Mikkeller Barrel Room**
**MAP F3 ■ Refshalevej 169B
■ 51 25 61 65 ■ Opening hours vary;
call to confirm**

A cavernous bar, taproom and concert venue specializing in barrel-aged beers, this forms part of Mikkel Borg Bjergsø's burgeoning beer empire. With panoramic views of Copenhagen harbour and regular street-food events, this is the perfect place to while away a sunny afternoon.

② **GoMonkey**
**MAP B2 ■ Vandtårnsvej 55,
Søborg ■ 25 53 30 22 ■ Open
10am–6pm daily**

Channel your inner Tarzan at this suburban climbing park in Søborg, which is a 15-minute train ride from central Copenhagen. There are ziplines, rope bridges, high-wires, as well as swing ropes.

③ **Meyers Madhus**
**MAP C3 ■ Nørrebrogade 52 C
■ 35 36 38 37 ■ Open 9am–4pm
Mon–Fri**

If you'd like to learn how to cook New Nordic, get schooled by the master himself at one of celebrity chef and restaurateur Claus Meyer's Nørrebro cookery classes. Large groups are welcome, but early booking is advised.

④ **Amager Strand Beach Park**
**MAP C3 ■ Amager Strand Promenaden
1 ■ 26 30 24 83 ■ Open May–Sep**

Boasting 2.9 miles (4.6 km) of beaches, a world-class skatepark and an open-air concert venue, this sprawling public beach park springs into life in May / June when sun-starved city-dwellers flock to the coast at the first sign of summer.

⑤ **Dragør Havn**
**MAP C3 ■ Dragør, south of
Copenhagen Airport**

It may be less than 7 miles (12 km) from central Copenhagen, but this charming fishing village and marina is a world away from the hustle and bustle of the city centre. The settlement dates back to the 12th century, and today still boasts a clutch of immaculately preserved medieval buildings in the traditional Danish style. In the evening, head down to the marina for excellent seafood at local restaurants.

Sailboats at Dragør marina

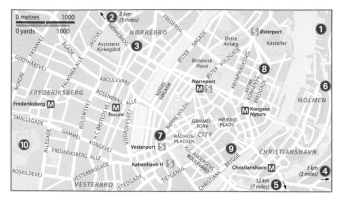

6 Noma "village"
Refshalevej 96 ■ 32 96 32 97 ■ Open noon–4pm, 6pm–12:30am Wed–Sat ■ www.noma.dk

An old mining depot on Refshaleøen – the next urban island to grow into a destination dining spot – has been beautifully preserved to provide a new home for the world-famous Noma restaurant (opening February 2018). The concept is a gastonomic village with different huts for different food preparation categories, plus an urban farm *(see p97)*.

7 Nordic Noir Tours
MAP D5 ■ Vesterport Station ■ nordicnoirtours.com

Discover the darker side of the city with a guided tour of the film locations used in hit crime dramas *Forbrydelsen (The Killing)*, *Borgen* and *The Bridge*. Take a peek behind the scenes at each series, and venture into some of the city's lesser-known spots. Tours start from Vesterport Station, and discounts are often offered on pre-bookings.

8 ExitGames
MAP L2 ■ Fredericiagade 30 ■ 60 54 30 37 ■ exitgamescph.dk

Put your sleuthing skills to the test at Copenhagen's premier live escape game, where you must find the hidden objects, figure out the clues and solve the puzzles to earn your freedom and escape from one of three film-themed rooms.

9 Royal Library Gardens
MAP K5 ■ Proviantpassagen 1 ■ Open 6am–10pm daily

Tucked away behind Christiansborg Palace on Slotsholmen island, this secluded public park was built in 1920 on the site of King Christian IV's former naval port. The fountain in the central pool cascades every hour in a nod to the garden's fascinating maritime heritage.

Sunbathing at Royal Library Gardens

10 Frederiksberg Have
Set against the dramatic backdrop of Frederiksberg Slot, this stunning romantic garden is an oasis of calm *(see p87)*. Between 1798 and 1802 the gardens were landscaped to reflect a typical English garden. Explore its lawns and canals and you might even be rewarded with a glimpse of the elephants at Zoologisk Have *(see p88)*.

⏏ Children's Attractions

Fun for the entire family on board the train at Tivoli

1 Tivoli
The best time to take kids to Tivoli is during the day, when the atmosphere is more family-oriented. The park's many fun rides include cars on tracks, dragon boats on the lake, the pantomime theatre and the trolley bus *(see pp14–15)*.

2 Guinness World Records Museum
This highly popular attraction brings the Guinness World Records to life. From the utterly bizarre, such as bicycle-eating men, to the internationally renowned in sport and

Guinness World Records Museum

science, 13 galleries celebrate strangeness, ingenuity and determination *(see p72)*.

3 World of H C Andersen Museum
Explore the life of Hans Christian Andersen at this charming museum *(see p72)*. It is aimed at kids, who will enjoy the tableaux and recordings of some of his fairy tales. The manuscript of *The Stone and the Wise Man* (1858) may interest bibliophiles.

4 Nationalmuseet
Copenhagen's National Museum *(see pp30–31)* includes an interesting Children's Museum where children are encouraged to participate in a range of activities, including dressing up in grandma's clothes to see how different they are from today's garments, or sitting in an old Danish classroom learning about medieval castles.

5 Bakken
MAP B2 ■ Dyrehavevej 62
■ 39 63 35 44 ■ www.bakken.dk
If you go down to the woods today... you'll find the world's oldest amusement park. Established in 1583, Bakken is a real one-off: a quirky mix of modern thrill rides and vintage sideshows that offers free entry all year round.

6 Experimentarium

MAP B2 ■ Tuborg Havnevej, Hellerup ■ 39 27 33 33 ■ Open 9:30am–5pm Mon–Fri (until 8pm Thu), 10am–5pm Sat–Sun ■ Adm; under-2s free ■ www.experimentarium.dk

This innovative science centre brings science to life via hands-on exploration. Most exhibits are interactive, allowing kids to perform over 300 experiments, and adults can have just as much fun as the kids too. Environmental issues are high on the agenda.

7 Statens Museum for Kunst

The Children's Art Museum at the National Gallery caters for children aged between 4 and 12, with work-shops where kids can draw, paint and sculpt, and there is also a sketching room. On the first Sunday of each month, the museum holds a family day, which includes guided museum tours (see pp26–7).

8 Zoologisk Have

This zoo is Denmark's largest cultural institution, attracting around 1.2 million visitors every year. Besides the tigers, polar bears and elephants, there are thematic adventure trails and a children's petting zoo. In spring, there tend to be many new baby animals (see p88).

9 Den Blå Planet

Denmark's national aquarium is the largest in Northern Europe, with over 20,000 marine life forms and seven million litres of water. The aquarium's architecture is certainly worthy of as much attention as its exhibits (see p100).

Marine life at Den Blå Planet

10 Fælledparken

Copenhagen's largest public park, in Østerbro next to the Danish National Stadium, has a fantastic playground featuring multiple tiny trampolines and castles. There is also a skatepark, cafés, sports fields and numerous green lawns for other activities. The park was created between 1906 and 1914 by landscape architect Edvard Glæsel (see p80).

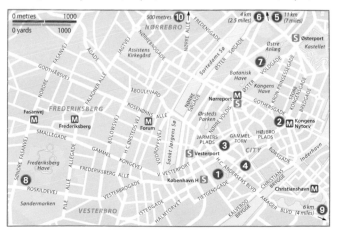

Performing Arts and Music Venues

Tables at Wallmans Cirkusbygningen

1 Wallmans Cirkusbygningen
MAP G5 ■ Jernbanegade 8 ■ 33 16 37 00 ■ www.wallmans.dk
Built in 1884, this circular venue was previously a circus building. Today it is used as a glamorous setting for old-fashioned "dinner, show and dancing" evenings. The spectacular entertainment surrounds guests across seven stages while resting members of the cast serve dinner. After the show, it turns into a club.

2 Det Kongelige Teater
World-class performances of ballet are held in Kongens Nytorv *(see p23)*, while dramatic works are performed at the playhouse on the waterfront, Skuespilhuset.

Performance at Det Kongelige Teater

3 Operaen
Famed for its acoustics, the Opera House attracts a variety of international productions. You can enjoy a good view of the stage from any seat and all the seats are relatively cheap due to government subsidy *(see pp94–5)*.

4 Tivoli Concert Hall
The Tivoli Concert Hall is Copenhagen's largest music venue, with a capacity of 1,900. It stages over 100 operas, ballets and rock and jazz concerts during the Tivoli season *(see pp14–15)*.

5 Jazzhouse
MAP J4 ■ Niels Hemmingsens Gade 10 ■ 33 15 37 00 ■ www.jazzhouse.dk
Copenhagen's biggest venue for jazz, the Jazzhouse offers a unique, varied programme. On weekends, late-night concerts kick off at 11pm.

6 Mojo Bluesbar
MAP H5 ■ Løngangstræde 21C ■ 33 11 64 53 ■ www.mojo.dk
Smoky, small and intimate, this bar is known for its laid-back blues and live jazz performances. There won't be any distracting gimmicks here.

7 Det Ny Teater
MAP C5 ■ Gammel Kongevej 29 ■ 33 25 50 75 ■ www.detny teater.dk

This early 20th-century theatre hosts a variety of popular international musicals, such as *Phantom of the Opera* and *Les Misérables*.

8 Koncerthuset
MAP B3 ■ Ørestads Boulevard 13 ■ 35 20 62 62 ■ www.dr.dk/ koncerthuset

The concert house of the national broadcaster Danmarks Radio (DR) was designed by Jean Nouvel. This landmark building with its blue glass façade has superior acoustics.

Koncerthuset's curved interior

9 Parken
MAP D2 ■ Per Henrik Lings Allé 2 ■ 35 43 31 31 ■ www.teliaparken.dk

This football stadium held its first concert in 2001 with the Eurovision Song Contest. Bands including U2 and Metallica have since performed.

10 VEGA
MAP B6 ■ Enghavevej 40 ■ 33 25 70 11 ■ Club nights: 11pm–4am Fri and Sat; adm: 60 Dkr after 1am ■ www.vega.dk

Occupying a 1950s trade union building, VEGA offers club nights that attract international acts and DJs.

TOP 10 JAZZ VENUES AND EVENTS

Copenhagen Jazz Festival

1 Copenhagen Jazz Festival/ Winter Jazz
In February and July Copenhagen hosts Scandinavia's biggest jazz festival.

2 Charlie Scott's
MAP H4 ■ Skindergade 43 ■ 33 12 12 20
Tiny city-centre bar for jazz lovers.

3 Jazzhus Montmartre
MAP K3 ■ Store Renegade 19a ■ 31 72 34 94
This legendary venue seats 70 people.

4 La Fontaine
MAP J5 ■ Kompagnistræde 11 ■ 33 11 60 98
Known for late sessions Fri and Sat.

5 Huset-KBH
MAP J5 ■ Rådhusstræde 13 ■ 21 51 21 51
Culture house hosts a jazz club.

6 Jazzcup
MAP J3 ■ Gothersgade 107 ■ 33 15 02 02
Both a record store and a café hosting jazz sessions on weekends.

7 Sofie Kælderen
MAP L6 ■ Overgaden Oven Vandet 32 ■ 32 57 77 01
A cornerstone of Copenhagen's jazz scene, attracting big names in jazz.

8 Tango y Vinos
MAP L4 ■ Herluf Trolles Gade 9 ■ 33 32 81 16
Tiny Argentinian wine bar hosting jazz, flamenco, funk and tango musicians.

9 Kind of Blue
MAP D3 ■ Ravnsborggade 17 ■ 26 35 10 56
A recent addition to the city's jazz scene.

10 Palæ Bar
MAP K4 ■ Ny Adelgade 5 ■ 33 12 54 71
A favourite hangout for musicians.

⁝⁝⁝ Nightlife Venues

Plush, subterranean interior of Copenhagen speakeasy The Jane

1 The Jane
MAP J4 ■ Gråbrødretorv 8
■ 61 69 21 64 ■ Open 8pm–5am
Thu–Sat ■ www.thejane.dk

A night at this part wood-panelled speakeasy, part industrial nightclub is whatever you want it to be. Chat over classic cocktails and soft jazz in the library bar, or cut loose on the hidden dance floor, neatly accessed via a false bookcase.

2 Hive
MAP H4 ■ Skindergade 45–7
■ 28 45 74 67 ■ Open 11pm–6am
Fri and Sat ■ www.hive.dk

The city's old courthouse is now a modern nightclub complete with iPhone chargers at the tables.

3 Rust
Trendy Rust is at the cutting edge of the local music and clubbing scene. It showcases up-and-coming acts, live music sets and top international DJs (see p82).

4 Brass Monkey
MAP B6 ■ Enghavevej 31
■ Open 8pm–1am Thu, 8pm–3am
Fri and Sat ■ www.brassmonkey.dk

Swap the stresses of city life for plastic paradise at Copenhagen's Tiki bar, a kitsch wonderland of exotic cocktails, grass skirts and hula girls.

5 KB3
MAP C6 ■ Kødboderne 3
■ 33 23 45 97 ■ Open 11pm–late
Thu–Sat ■ www.kb3.dk

Housed in a former abattoir, this superclub provides the soundtrack to the meatpacking district's weekend nightlife. The club's backyard is used for open-air parties in the summer.

6 Bakken
MAP C6 ■ Flæsketorvet 19–21
■ Open 9pm–5am Thu, 6pm–5am Fri and Sat ■ www.bakkenkbh.dk

Not to be confused with the children's theme park in Dyrehaven, this dark, dingy and achingly hip club is a cornerstone of Copenhagen's underground music scene.

Revellers at Bakken

(7) Ideal Bar

MAP B6 ■ Enghavevej 40 ■ 33 25 70 11 ■ Open 8pm–1am selected Weds, 9pm–2am Thu, 10pm– 5am Fri and Sat ■ www.idealbar.vega.dk

On the ground floor of trendy venue VEGA (see p55), this lounge bar offers club nights with a local vibe. It is an inexpensive midweek option.

(8) Culture Box

MAP K2 ■ Kronprinsessegade 54 ■ 33 32 50 50 ■ Open 11pm–6am Fri and Sat (Cocktail Box open from 9pm) ■ Closed Jun–Jul ■ Min age 18 ■ www.culture-box.com

This purist techno club is one of Copenhagen's leading venues for electronic music. Its cocktail bar opens earlier than the club and makes a good meeting place.

DJ at work, Culture Box

(9) Hornsleth

MAP J4 ■ Lovstraede 4 ■ Open 9pm–4am Fri and Sat ■ www. hornslethbar.dk

Not for the prudish, this decadent superclub is a shrine to provocative Danish artist Kristian von Hornsleth. The music, however, is less daring, with DJs spinning a reliable mix of club classics.

(10) Gefährlich

Located in the heart of Nørrebro, known for its club culture, Gefährlich (German for "dangerous") has a restaurant, bar, art gallery, coffee shop, boutique and record store. Its nightclub caters to the tastes of the young and hip (see p82).

TOP 10 MICROBREWERIES

The beer menu at Warpigs

1 Warpigs
MAP C5 ■ Fuglebækvej 2C ■ 32 50 62 00 ■ www.amagerbryghus.dk
Tours Mon–Sat by appointment.

2 Nørrebro Bryghus
MAP D3 ■ Ryesgade 3, Nørrebro ■ 35 30 05 30 ■ www.noerrebrobryghus.dk
Tour this brewery and taste some beer.

3 Vesterbro Bryghus
MAP H5 ■ Vesterbrogade 2B ■ 33 11 17 05 ■ www.vesterbrobryghus.dk
Six Austrian recipe beer brews.

4 BRUS
MAP C3 ■ Guldbergsgade 29 ■ 75 22 22 00 ■ www.tapperietbrus.dk
With 33 beers on tap and an on-site restaurant, this slick brewpub has it all.

5 Brewpub
MAP H5 ■ Vestergade 29 ■ 33 32 00 60 ■ Closed Sun ■ www.brewpub.dk
This place has a lovely 17th-century beer garden.

6 Bryggeriet Apollo
MAP G5 ■ Vesterbrogade 3 ■ 33 12 33 13 ■ www.bryggeriet.dk
The original local microbrewery.

7 Ølsnedkeren
MAP C4 ■ Griffenfeldsgade 52 ■ 22 55 28 70 ■ www.olsnedkeren.dk
Everything here is made on site.

8 Bryggeri Skovlyst
MAP B2 ■ Skovlystvej 2, Værløse ■ 44 98 65 45
A microbrewery with a restaurant.

9 Mikkeller
Viktoriagade 8, Vesterbro ■ 33 31 04 15 ■ www.mikkeller.dk
Set up in 2006, this has its own pub.

10 Copenhagen Beer Festival
Tap 1, Ny Carlsbergvej 91, Vesterbro ■ www.copenhagenbeerfest.com
Beer festival held each May and Sep.

🔟 Gay and Lesbian Venues

① Centralhjørnet
MAP H4 ■ Kattesundet 18
■ 33 11 85 49 ■ Open noon–2am
Sun–Thu, noon–3am Fri & Sat ■ www.
centralhjornet.dk

This is Copenhagen's oldest gay bar, dating from 1852. It holds drag nights; regular shows take place on Thursdays. Kylie Minogue and Europop are jukebox favourites. Sunday afternoons are usually packed with people dancing.

Drinks at Masken Bar & Café

② Jailhouse
MAP H4 ■ Studiestræde 12
■ 33 15 22 55 ■ Open 3pm–2am
Sun–Thu, 3pm–5am Fri & Sat;
Restaurant: 6–9pm Wed–Fri
■ www.jailhousecph.dk

Kitted out as a prison, this café and event bar has booths like prison cells and staff dressed as prison guards or police officers. There is a restaurant on the second floor; the atmosphere here is relaxed.

③ Oscar Bar and Café
MAP H5 ■ Rådhuspladsen 77 ■
33 12 09 99 ■ Open 11am–11pm Sun–Thu, 11am–2am Fri–Sat (kitchen until 4pm daily) ■ www.oscarbarcafe.dk

A cosy evening bar and café for the style-conscious, with a long bar and posh leather furniture. The DJ plays funky disco and soulful deep house at the weekends.

Seating at Oscar Bar and Café

④ Masken Bar & Café
MAP H4 ■ Studiestræde 33
■ 33 91 09 37 ■ Open 2pm–3am
Sun–Thu, 2pm–5am Fri and Sat
■ www.maskenbar.dk

This venue has exciting live music and drag shows.

⑤ Café Intime
MAP B5 ■ Allégade 25, 2000
Frederiksberg ■ 38 34 19 58 ■ Open
6pm–2am daily ■ www.cafeintime.dk

Founded in 1913, this kitsch bar has a predominantly gay crowd. A pianist plays popular classics; you can also enjoy jazz on Sundays.

⑥ Amigo Bar
MAP C5 ■ Schønbergsgade 4
(corner of Gammel Kongevej), 2000
Frederiksberg ■ 33 21 49 15 ■ Open
10pm–7am daily

This popular bar has a lively party atmosphere into the early hours.

7 Mens Bar
MAP H4 ■ Teglgårdsstræde 3
■ 33 12 73 03 ■ Open 3pm–2am daily
■ www.mensbar.dk

This strictly all-male, no-frills bar is filled with leather, fascinating tattoos and a dash of denim. Try to catch the free Danish brunch at 3pm on the first Sunday of the month.

8 Never Mind Bar
MAP G4 ■ Nørre Voldgade
■ Open 10pm–6am daily ■ www.nevermindbar.dk

The party rarely stops here at this popular, central LGBT nightclub. If the party is still rocking at 6am, the bartenders will keep the alcohol flowing. There are several dance floors where you can show off your moves. No dress code.

9 Meet Gay Copenhagen
27 21 80 65 ■ www.meetgaycopenhagen.dk

You can meet and dine with local gays and lesbians in the comfort of their homes. Hosts are very friendly and usually offer traditional fare. Note: this is not a dating agency.

10 Vela
MAP C5 ■ Viktoriagade 2–4
■ 33 14 34 19 ■ Open 9pm–midnight Wed, 9pm–4am Thu, 9pm–5am Fri and Sat ■ www.velagayclub.dk

Attracting a mixed crowd, Vela is a popular lesbian bar with oriental decor in the Vesterbro area. There's table football, small booths and a selection of cheap beers.

TOP 10 GAY AND LESBIAN FESTIVALS AND EVENTS

Copenhagen Pride Festival

1 Torchlight Procession
May ■ www.aidsfondet.dk
This event in memory of people who have died of AIDS takes place on the last Sunday in May.

2 St Hans
23 Jun ■ www.copenhagen-gay-life.dk
Annual bonfire and beach party on Amager Beach on Sankt Hans Night.

3 Queer Festival
Late Jul ■ www.queerfestival.org
Musicians, activists and drag kings and queens.

4 Malmö Pride Festival
Aug ■ www.malmopride.com
Across the bridge, this jamboree was previously called the Rainbow Festival.

5 Copenhagen Pride Festival
Aug ■ www.copenhagenpride.dk
Week-long festival in August. Includes the gay pride parade.

6 Mix Copenhagen Film Festival
Oct ■ www.mixcopenhagen.dk
Ten-day lesbian, gay, bi and trans film festival held annually in October.

7 World Aids Day
■ 1 Dec
Commemorated each year.

8 Nordic Open
30 Dec ■ www.pandans.dk/nordicopen.htm
A popular dance contest for same-sex couples held each year.

9 GAY CPH App
For more events while exploring the city, download this free app.

10 Pan Idræt
www.panidraet.dk
Gay and lesbian sports club for a variety of activites, including badminton, swimming and rugby.

TOP10 Restaurants

Asian-inspired furniture and tropical flowers at Kiin Kiin

1 Relæ

Talented chef Christian Puglisi was the first Noma-alumnus to make it big, earning his own Michelin star. Diners flock to this minimal space in Nørrebro to experience an affordable yet remarkable balance of flavours and textures in a completely unfussy environment *(see p83)*.

2 Aamann's 1921

Copenhagen's *smørrebrød* (open sandwich) king serves arguably the best sandwiches in town, and reinvents Danish dinner by remixing the usual inputs in unusual combinations. From fried chicken with lingonberries to shrimp on toast made from house-ground flour, this kitchen is rewardingly obsessed with detail *(see p75)*.

3 Kadeau

Everything served at this relaxed yet beautifully designed spot in Christianshavn is grown on the fertile Danish island Bornholm. The impressive, seasonal 15-course menu deftly weaves foraged botanical delicacies, such as woodruff and wild carrots, into unforgettable unions with the finest seafood and meat *(see p97)*.

4 Kiin Kiin

Dining at Europe's only Michelin-starred Thai restaurant is a feast for the senses. Start by sipping Champagne and scoffing street food in the underground snug, and then follow your nose upstairs to the lemongrass and bamboo-scented dining room for a masterclass in modern Thai cooking *(see p83)*.

5 Era Ora

This Michelin-star eatery has been hailed as the world's best Italian restaurant outside of Italy, and the best restaurant of 2017, by respected foodie magazine *Gambero Rosso*. Ingredients are imported from Italy for authenticity, and prepared according to time-honoured tradition. The impressive wine cellar, meanwhile, houses some 75,000 bottles and 700 labels *(see p97)*.

6 Formel B

Beautifully prepared, French-style cuisine using fresh Danish ingredients is the key to the tasty dishes served in this charming restaurant, which prides itself on supporting animal welfare and sustainability. Sample raw marinated shrimps with squid and soy-ginger browned butter *(see p91)*.

Pretty plate at Formel B

7 108

Sister restaurant to Noma, 108 earned its own stars by pushing the flavour boundaries of Nordic gastronomy. With reasonable prices and a cool perch on the canal, 108 and its adjoining café, which serves coffee, wine and small plates, are buzzing all day *(see p97)*.

8 Bror

The Danish word for 'brother', Bror prides itself on honest comfort food created with innovative flair. This ethos is reflected in the restaurant's simple decor – it has a muted colour palate punctuated with fauna and wooden furniture. The two chefs, both formerly sous chefs at Noma, create punchy Nordic dishes, such as veal shank braised overnight and a bone marrow crème brûlée *(see p75)*.

Tables at Kong Hans Kælder

9 Kong Hans Kælder

This unique restaurant is set in Copenhagen's oldest building, offering a wonderful atmosphere beneath its vaulted ceiling. Choose to eat from either the à la carte or fixed-price menu and watch the skilled chef at work in the open kitchen *(see p75)*.

10 Søllerød Kro

This Michelin-star countryside inn is a wonderful retreat away from the hubbub of central Copenhagen. The beautiful interiors are matched by a standout menu that once more highlights the Danes' creative flair with flavours. A tasting menu is available with carefully chosen wine pairings *(see p105)*.

TOP 10 DANISH CAFÉS AND BARS

The quirky Laundromat Café

1 Laundromat Café
MAP C3 ▪ Elmegade 15, Nørrebro
Enjoy a coffee while doing your laundry.

2 Coffee Collective
MAP H3 ▪ Vendersgade 6D
From farmer, to roaster, to barista, the Collective crafts the ultimate coffee.

3 Mad og Kaffe
MAP C6 ▪ Sønder Boulevard 68
The most popular café in the city is famous for colourful brunches.

4 Bo-Bi Bar
MAP J4 ▪ Klareboderne 4
Since 1917, artists and office drones have visited this tiny room to talk beer.

5 Øl & Bread
MAP C5 ▪ Viktoriagade 6
This "beer & bread" bar matches its impressive *smørrebrød* line-up to rotating taps of Mikkeller beers.

6 Ruby
MAP J5 ▪ Nybrogade 10
One of the world's top 50 cocktail bars, situated on the canal.

7 La Glace
MAP H4 ▪ Skoubogade 3–5
La Glace is one of the foremost confectioneries in Copenhagen.

8 Brus
MAP C3 ▪ Guldbergsgade 29
This quirky little café roasts all of its beans on the premises.

9 The Corner
MAP M4 ▪ Strandgade 108
Gorgeous house-made pastries and coffee each morning; New Nordic small plates and wine by day.

10 Lidkoeb
MAP C5 ▪ Vesterbrogade 72B
Drinking den in a former apothecary; cocktail bar and whisky house.

Shopping Districts

1 Kronprinsensgade
MAP J4

This posh shopping area includes many of Scandinavia's top designer brands, such as Stig P and Le-Fix. You will also find Scandinavia's oldest tea shop, Perch's Tea Room.

2 Off Strøget (South)
MAP J4–J5

The streets to the south of Strøget are great for "alternative" shopping. Læderstræde and Kompagnistræde are especially good, the latter mostly for its antique shops.

3 Off Strøget (North)
MAP H4–J4

Heading up north from Strøget, you will find numerous little boutiques, record stores and second-hand shops. Go shopping on streets like Skindergade, Larsbjørnstræde, Vestergade and Studiestræde.

4 Strøget
MAP H5–K4

Copenhagen's shopping street is known as "the walking street". The shops, which stretch across five linked pedestrian streets, range from cheerful and inexpensive outlets to designer and upmarket department stores (towards Kongens Nytorv), with something for everyone.

Airy interior of the Fisketorvet mall

5 Fisketorvet Copenhagen Mall
MAP D6 ■ Kalvebod Brygge 59, Havneholmen 5, Vesterbro ■ 35 37 19 17 ■ Open 10am–8pm Mon–Fri, 10am–6pm Sat & Sun

On the waterfront facing the Inner Harbour, this city mall is minutes away from the Copencabana harbour pool. It has more than 120 shops, several restaurants and a cinema.

6 Vesterbro
MAP C5–C6

This former red-light area is now an offbeat shopping district offering

Window-shopping along Copenhagen's famous shopping street, Strøget

some very good bargains. Among the more interesting streets in the neighbourhood are Istedgade, which is lined with boutiques and art shops, and Værnedamsvej, which has several independent fashion stores and gourmet food shops.

7 Nansensgade
MAP G3

Located on the outskirts of the old town, this area has a mix of traditional and trendy boutiques, as well as good restaurants and cafés.

8 Torvehallerne KBH
MAP H3

Food-lovers are in for a treat at Copenhagen's covered market on Israels Plads, with gourmet food stands, takeout delights and delicious delis.

Seafood stall at Torvehallerne KBH

9 Nørrebro
MAP C3–D3

Not as trendy as it once was, but Nørrebro still has many second-hand stores and chic boutiques. Head to Ravnsborggade for antiques, Jaegersborggade for the offbeat and Elmegade for vintage clothes.

10 Bredgade
MAP L3

If you are looking for traditional, pre-20th-century antiques, this is the perfect place to visit. Here you will find several grand-looking shops and auction houses that sell all kinds of antiques, including authentic paintings and statues.

TOP 10 DANISH DESIGN COMPANIES

Georg Jensen silverware

1 Georg Jensen Silverware
www.georgjensen.com
Original, organic tableware designs and casual jewellery.

2 Cylinda-Line (by Arne Jacobsen)
www.stelton.dk
Popular tableware collection (1967) in steel, wood and plastic.

3 Bang & Olufsen
www.bang-olufsen.com
Known for their cutting-edge audio-visual designs.

4 Kaare Klint Furniture
Combines ergonomics with elegant 18th-century English styles.

5 Bodum
www.bodum.com
Classic and smart kitchenware in steel and glass.

6 LEGO®
www.lego.com
These popular building blocks were introduced in 1952.

7 Vipp
www.vipp.com
Designers of a classic stainless steel pedal bin, Vipp's products also include soap dishes and dispensers.

8 Royal Copenhagen
www.royalcopenhagen.com
Royal porcelain design featuring famous Flora Danica motifs.

9 Poul Henningsen Lamps
Lamp design creating the effect of maximum light and minimum shadow.

10 Kjærholm Furniture
Poul Kjærholm-designed functional coffee tables and chairs, all named simply PK with a number. Production continues under the leadership of his son, Thomas.

Copenhagen for Free

The Royal Botanical Gardens

1 Botanisk Have

Take a stroll through this green oasis in the heart of the city, which boasts stunning glasshouses, gardens and over 13,000 species of plantlife. Behind the scenes, the garden's botanists develop scientific collections of rare plants and fungi, making them available for research, teaching and the public (see p78).

2 Visit world-class museums
www.natmus.dk

All of the city's national museums, including Nationalmuseet (see pp30–31) and the Statens Museum for Kunst (see pp26–7), are free for under-18s, while many city-centre institutions offer free entry for adults one day per week – check the relevant website for specific days.

3 Watch an open-air movie
MAP D2 ■ Edel Sauntes Allé ■ www.zulu.dk

It doesn't get much more cosy and *hygge* than this: every summer, Zulu brings its open-air cinema to Fælledparken, a sprawling public park in Østerbro. All you need to do is bring a blanket.

4 Havnebadet
MAP E6 ■ Islands Brygge 14 ■ www.teambade.kk.dk

On hot days, Copenhageners flock to this open-air swimming bath. There are five pools in all, while three diving towers give thrillseekers the opportunity to show off their stunts.

5 A Harbourside Promenade

Make the obligatory visit to the Little Mermaid (see p13) on foot, and then continue inland into Kastellet, the historic green fortress that is still a working military barracks, before exploring the Gefion Fountain and St Alban's Church (see p80).

6 Den Sorte Diamant
MAP K5 ■ Søren Kierkegaards Plads 1

Not only does this eye-catching modern extension of the Royal Library house every book ever printed in Danish (some six million), it's also home to the very good National Museum of Photography.

7 Changing of the guard at Amalienborg Palace

Come rain or shine, the Royal Life Guards stoically stand watch outside Amalienborg Palace (see pp24–5). Every day at noon, you can watch them march through the city.

⑧ Christiansborg Tårnet

At 106 m (348 ft), the tower on Christiansborg Palace *(see pp32–3)* is the highest point in Copenhagen's historic centre, and offers great views of the city. Space on the viewing platform is limited, so expect to queue for the elevator.

⑨ Explore Christiania

A maze of hippy hangouts and Hobbit-like homes, this self-declared "freetown" has been a counter-culture haven for dreamers and anarchists for over 40 years *(see pp28–9)*.

Communal area in Christiania

⑩ Absalon

MAP C6 ■ Sønder Blvd 73 ■ Open 7am–midnight daily ■ www.absaloncph.dk

Hang out with locals at this centre offering free activities for all the family. Show off your ping-pong prowess, dance the tango or try some traditional Danish cooking.

Guards outside Amalienborg Palace

TOP 10 BUDGET TIPS

Street food outlet

1 Try street food
Fast-food outlets are plentiful, and street-food outlets offer substantial, high-quality dishes for 100 Dkr or less.

2 Get Outdoors
Walking the streets is free and fascinating, while public parks and gardens (except Tivoli) are free, and often host free entertainment.

3 See a play
MAP K4 ■ Tordenskjoldsgade 7
The Danish National Theatre sells unsold tickets at half price after 4pm on the day of the performance.

4 Buy a Copenhagen Card
The Copenhagen Card offers transport and sightseeing discounts *(see p112)*.

5 Free walking tours
There are several walking tour operators that provide expert tips as well as sight information. A tip is expected at the end of the tour.

6 Have a big breakfast
Eat-all-you-want breakfasts offer good value for money, even at 100–150 Dkr.

7 Don't worry about tipping
Tips are usually included in bills at restaurants, hotels and taxis.

8 Free outdoor concerts
Every Wednesday in the spring and summer, students from the Royal Danish Academy of Music perform classical concerts at the Teatermuseet.

9 Try ice-skating
Free skating is on offer at rinks at Toftegård Plads in Valby, Frederiksberg Runddel and Blågårds Plads.

10 Dine outside
Barbecues, picnics and alcohol are allowed in most public parks across Copenhagen, ideal for dining alfresco.

Copenhagen
Area by Area

A view across the iconic rooftops
of Copenhagen's old city

10 Tivoli North to Gothersgade

Rich in history and culture, this area is a popular entertainment destination. Heading northeast of Tivoli, which was originally outside the city walls, you can walk back in time through the old town that evolved during the Middle Ages – though much of it succumbed to fire in the 18th century – to Slotsholmen, the site where the first dwellings that became the city of Copenhagen were built in the 12th century. Along the way, you will find great shopping areas, museums, an old town and a truly wonderful royal palace.

Christian V Statue

TIVOLI NORTH TO GOTHERSGADE

Astronomical clock on display

1 Astronomical Clock
MAP H5 ■ Rådhus,
Rådhuspladsen 1 ■ 33 66 25 86
■ Open 8:30am–4pm Mon–Fri,
10am–1pm Sat ■ Adm

This clock shows local time, solar
time, sunrise and sunset times,
celestial pole movement and the
movement of the planets.

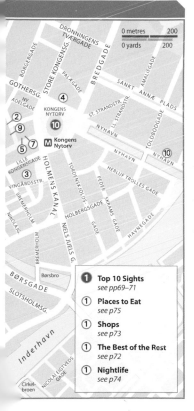

2 Kunstforeningen Gammel Strand
MAP J4 ■ Gammel Strand 48 ■ 33 36
02 60 ■ Open 11am–5pm Tue–Sun
(until 8pm Wed) ■ Adm; free with
Copenhagen Card ■ www.glstrand.dk

The Gammel Strand art association
was formed in 1825. The centre puts
on five to six changing exhibitions
annually, from group shows to retro-
spectives, both classic and contemporary. There is also an excellent
bookshop on the first floor and a
pleasant café. To gain disabled
access you must walk through the
courtyard at Læderstræde 15.

3 Tivoli
A park that has virtually
become synonymous with
Copenhagen, Tivoli should be high
on the list for any visitor to the city
(see pp14–15). Any season, this park
buzzes with the sounds of exhilarating
rides. It is not only for adventure-
seekers though. At night, the setting
turns quite magical and romantic,
with fairy lights and Japanese lanterns
glowing in the darkness. There's
often live music, too.

Flowers in bloom at Tivoli

4 Latin Quarter
To the west of Strøget lies
the Latin Quarter (see pp18–19), the
original home of the University of
Copenhagen. It dates back to the
Middle Ages when the primary language of education was Latin. Some
of the old university buildings are
used, although much of the campus
is now on the island of Amager.

5 Amagertorv
MAP J4

This busy square is in the middle of Strøget *(see p62)*. Note the attractive tiles designed by Bjørn Nørgaard. The square's focal point, the lovely Storkespringvandet fountain, provided the inspiration for a Danish folk song of the 1960s, and today is a popular meeting place. The cafés Norden and Europa, on either side of the square, are always buzzing.

6 Slotsholmen

A visit to Slotsholmen could take up almost an entire day, as there is plenty to see. It is primarily the site of Christiansborg Slot *(see pp32–3)*, which burnt down in 1794, but was rebuilt and is now home to Denmark's Parliament; it is also used by the Queen for State functions (visit the State Rooms on a guided tour). Museums here include the Tøjhusmuseet, filled with historic arms and armour, and the delightful Teatermuseet *(see p44)* featuring the 18th-century palace theatre. Other sights include the palace church and the 12th-century ruins of the first Copenhagen castle where the city's founder, Bishop Absalon, resided.

7 Ny Carlsberg Glyptotek
MAP H6 ■ Dantes Plads 7
■ 33 41 81 41 ■ Open 11am–6pm Tue–Sun (until 10pm Thu) ■ Adm; free with Copenhagen Card ■ www. glyptoteket.com

This superb art gallery is home to a collection of Mediterranean, classical and Egyptian art and artifacts. Danish and

Statues at Ny Carlsberg Glyptotek

19th-century French works of art are also on display, including splendid French Impressionist paintings *(see p44)*. The museum is housed in a 19th-century building with a cupola, beneath which lies an indoor winter garden, sculptures and water features. The modern wing is a wonderful area filled with light.

8 Rådhus
MAP H5 ■ Rådhuspladsen 1
■ 33 66 25 86 ■ Open 9am–4pm Mon–Fri, 9:30am–1pm Sat ■ Tours in English at 1pm Mon–Fri, 10am Sat; tower tour 11am & 2pm Mon–Fri, noon Sat ■ Adm for tours and tower

The Rådhus, or town hall, is a mock-Gothic building replete with fantastical sea creatures, built between 1892 and 1905 and designed by architect Martin Nyrop. Its tower affords superb views of the city. Take a tour, or just pop in to

Copenhagen's Rådhus

see the pre-Raphaelitesque entrance way, or the Italianate reception hall. Many Copenhageners get married here, so you may see several wedding parties on the town hall steps.

(9) Nationalmuseet

The National Museum is housed inside a former royal residence, dating from the 18th century. The exhibits trace Danish history, from ancient times to the present, including some amazing ethnographic collections. The most popular exhibits chart the history of Danes from the Ice Age to the Viking campaigns *(see pp30–31)*.

(10) Kongens Nytorv and Nyhavn

At the top of Nyhavn stands Kongens Nytorv or the King's New Square, an elegant area surrounded by fashionable 18th-century mansions that house banks, up-market department stores and hotels. The picturesque square (disrupted by Cityringen metro construction until 2019) is flanked by Charlottenborg Slot (now an exhibition space and home to the academy of art) and Det Kongelige Teater or Royal Theatre. Nyhavn (meaning "new harbour") is a lively area filled with restaurants, cafés and old sailing boats along the canal quayside. The atmosphere here is a stark contrast to what it was in the 1670s, when sailors, traders and low-lifes frequented the area. When Hans Christian Andersen lived here it was a red-light district. Even until the 1970s, this was not a part of town that many would have visited at night *(see pp22–3)*.

A WALKING TOUR OF THE AREA

▶ MORNING

Start your day's ramble at the **Ny Carlsberg Glyptotek**; don't miss the impressive Egyptian and Impressionist collections. Have an early lunch at the museum's charming Winter Garden Café *(Dantes Plads 7)*.

AFTERNOON

After lunch, cross H C Andersen Boulevard and head to the **Nationalmuseet** to take one of the hour-long tours. Stroll to the end of Ny Vestergade until you reach Frederiks Kanal. Cross the bridge and spend some time at **Christiansborg Slot** *(see pp32–3)*. If you arrive by 2pm, pop into the stables, the **Teatermuseet** *(see p44)* and the ruins before taking a tour of the State Rooms at 3pm. Then, walk back over the bridge and turn right onto Gammel Strand (note the **Fiskerkone**, *see p41*) for afternoon snacks at one of the restaurants and cafés. Walk **Købmagergade** via Højbro Plads, right up to **Rundetårn** *(see pp18–19)*. If you are feeling energetic, hike to the top for a good view of the city. Heading back down, take a left on to **Strøget** and keep walking until you reach **Kongens Nytorv and Nyhavn** – a perfect spot for an evening drink and supper at one of the quayside bars and restaurants. Instead of heading back via Strøget, take the less mainstream **Læderstræde**. Walk to **Rådhuspladsen** and go across to **Tivoli** *(see pp14–15)*. Spend the evening at these lovely gardens enjoying the atmosphere.

See map on pp68–9

The Best of the Rest

 Caritas Springvandet
MAP H4 ▪ Gammel Torv

Dating back to 1608, the Charity Fountain is one of the city's oldest.

2 Københavns Museum
MAP H5 ▪ Stormgade 18 ▪ See website for opening times ▪ Adm ▪ www.cphmuseum.kk.dk

The City Museum takes visitors on a journey through urban history, from the original settlers to today.

 Rådhuspladsen
MAP H5

At the end of Strøget, the town hall square is one of the liveliest areas.

 Strøget
MAP H5–K4

This is the name given to the five main, interconnected shopping streets of Copenhagen (see p62).

5 Guinness World Records Museum
MAP K4 ▪ Østergade 16 ▪ 33 32 31 31 ▪ Open Sep–mid-Jun: 10am–6pm daily (until 8pm Fri & Sat); mid-Jun–Aug: 10am–10pm daily ▪ Adm (combined tickets available) ▪ www.ripleys.com/copenhagen

As the name suggests, 500 Guinness World Records are displayed here (see p52).

6 World of H C Andersen Museum
MAP H5 ▪ Rådhuspladsen 57 ▪ 33 32 31 31 ▪ Open Sep–mid-Jun: 10am–6pm daily (until 8pm Fri–Sat); mid-Jun–Aug: 10am–10pm daily ▪ Adm ▪ www.ripleys.com/copenhagen

Scenes from Andersen's fairy tales are found here, plus other memorabilia.

Caritas Fountain

7 Grand Teatret
MAP H5 ▪ Mikkel Bryggers Gade 8 ▪ 33 15 16 11 ▪ www.grandteatret.dk

A historic six-screen cinema with some incredibly comfy seats and an excellent café, this is the film buffs' go-to place for international and arthouse movies.

8 Statue of H C Andersen
MAP H5 ▪ H C Andersens Boulevard

This statue of the author by Henry Lukow-Nielsen dates from 1961.

 **9 Georg Jensen Museum**
MAP J4 ▪ Amagertorv 4 ▪ 33 14 02 29 ▪ Open 10am–6pm Mon–Thu, 10am–7pm Fri, 10am–5pm Sat (Jun–Sep: Sun) ▪ www.georgjensen.com

The jewellery and homeware of the famous silversmith are on display at this wonderful museum.

10 Gammel Strand
MAP J4

This canalside street is home to excellent restaurants, one of the city's best flea markets and the Kunstforeningen Gammel Strand (see p69), an admirable art museum. It is also a pick-up point for Stromma Canal Tours (see p13).

People enjoying a Stromma Canal Tour

Shops

① **Illums Bolighus**
MAP J4 ▪ Amagertorv 10 ▪ 33 14 19 41 ▪ www.illumsbolighus.dk
This shrine to stylish interior design and kitchenware (mainly Italian and Danish) offers everything from Royal Copenhagen porcelain to groovy dog-biscuit dispensers and objets d'art.

② **Georg Jensen**
MAP J4 ▪ Amagertorv 4 ▪ 33 11 40 80 ▪ www.georgjensen.com
Georg Jensen's superb designs are available at the historic firm's flagship store. These include stylish jewellery, watches, cutlery, candlesticks, antiques and designer sunglasses.

③ **ILLUM**
MAP K4 ▪ Østergade 52 ▪ 33 14 40 02 ▪ www.illum.dk
A stylish, six storeyed department store offering quality clothing and homeware. There are also several cafés, a bakery and a supermarket.

④ **Birger Christensen**
MAP K4 ▪ Østergade 38 ▪ 33 11 55 55 ▪ www.birger-christensen.com
This fashion store sells Birger Christensen coats and jackets, as well as international labels.

⑤ **Royal Copenhagen Porcelain**
MAP J4 ▪ Amagertorv 6 ▪ 33 13 71 81 ▪ www. royalcopenhagen.com
This flagship store offers a range of designs, from the classic 18th-century *flora danica* design to the modern and organic.

A Royal Copenhagen fruit bowl

⑥ **Mads Nørgaard**
MAP J4 ▪ Amagertov 15 ▪ 33 32 01 28 ▪ www.madsnorgaard.com
Classic, casual Danish menswear is sold here, including the timeless trademark unisex striped top.

⑦ **Noa Noa**
MAP K4 ▪ Østergade 6 ▪ 29 74 31 66 ▪ www.noanoa.com/fr_fr
A contemporary Danish label that offers women's cottons, linens and silks in quirky, pretty styles. They also do a similar collection for girls aged 3–12.

Accessories on display at Hay House

⑧ **Hay House**
MAP K4 ▪ Østergade 61, 2nd Floor ▪ 42 82 08 20 ▪ www.hay.dk
In addition to the store on Pilestræde, a larger branch has opened above Café Norden on Amagertorv. Filled with bright plastic furniture and accessories.

⑨ **A Pair**
MAP K4 ▪ Ny Østergade 3 ▪ 33 91 99 20 ▪ www.apair.dk
Here you will find fashionable footwear for men and women, as well as leather bags and belts with large silver buckles. It is a chain with shops all over Denmark.

⑩ **Sand**
MAP K4 ▪ Østergade 40 ▪ 33 14 21 21 ▪ www.sand-europe.com
This Danish fashion house offers stylish and classic clothing and accessories for men and women.

See map on pp68–9

Nightlife

The cigar lounge at stylish restaurant The Jane

1 Ruby
MAP J5 ■ Nybrogade 10 ■ 33 93 12 03 ■ Open 4pm–2am Mon–Sat, 7pm–1am Sun ■ www.rby.dk

This exclusive bar is styled as an old-fashioned gentlemen's club.

2 Penthouse
MAP H4 ■ Nørregade 1 ■ 33 11 74 78 ■ Open 11pm–6am Fri & Sat ■ www.penthouse.nu

The entrance fee for this 1930s-style club includes unlimited soft drinks and draught beer.

3 Jazzhus Montmartre
MAP K3 ■ Store Regnegade 19A ■ 70 26 32 67 ■ Open 5:30–11:30pm Thu–Sat; concerts start at 8pm ■ Book ahead ■ Adm ■ www.jazzhusmontmartre.dk

A legendary jazz venue that attracts world-class jazz musicians.

4 Grand Teatret
MAP H5 ■ Mikkel Bryggers Gade 8 ■ 33 15 16 11 ■ www.grandteatret.dk

A large, six-screen arthouse cinema with a comfortable atmosphere and a small café.

5 Studenterhuset
MAP J3 ■ Købmagergade 52 ■ www.studenterhuset.com

This bar serves beer at discounted prices, and hosts local bands.

6 The Jane
MAP J4 ■ Gråbrødretorv 8 ■ 61 69 21 64 ■ Open 8pm–5am Thu–Sat ■ www.thejane.dk

Step into a Mad Men-esque world at this city-centre speakeasy.

7 Strøm
MAP J4 ■ Niels Hemmingsens Gade 32 ■ 81 18 94 21 ■ Open 6pm–12:30am Mon–Thu, 6pm–2.30am Fri & Sat ■ www.strombar.dk

This spit 'n' sawdust speakeasy serves up twists on classic cocktails.

8 Jazzhouse
MAP J4 ■ Niels Hemmingsens Gade 10 ■ 33 15 47 00 ■ Open from 7pm for concerts only ■ www.jazzhouse.dk

A live jazz venue attracting both international and local bands.

9 1105
MAP K4 ■ Kristen Bernikows Gade 4 ■ 33 93 11 05 ■ Open 8pm–2am Wed, Thu & Sat, 4pm–2am Fri ■ www.1105.dk

The bartenders at this hip cocktail bar mix the best drinks in the city.

10 Club Mambo
MAP H5 ■ Vester Voldgade 85 ■ 33 11 97 66 ■ Open 8pm–midnight Tue & Thu, 9pm–5am Fri & Sat ■ www.clubmambo.dk

Dance to salsa in this popular club.

→ *See map on pp68–9*

Places to Eat

① Aamann's 1921
MAP J4 ■ Niels Hemmingsens
Gade 19–21 ■ 20 80 52 04 ■ Open
11:30am–11pm daily (closed dinner
Sun & Mon) ■ www.aamanns.
dk/aamanns-1921 ■ Ⓚ

Rooted in traditional
Danish fare, Aamann's
offers an innovative
interpretation of
classic Danish
smørrebrød (see p60).

② L'Alsace
MAP K4 ■ Ny
Østergade 9 ■ 33 14 57 43
■ Closed Sun & public
holidays ■ www.alsace.dk
■ ⒦⒦

**Rhubarb and
verbena at Bror**

This classy restaurant specializes in
dishes from Alsace, with an emphasis
on fresh fish and seafood.

③ Kong Hans Kælder
MAP K4 ■ Vingårdsstræde 6
■ 33 11 68 68 ■ Open Mon–Sat D
■ www.konghans.dk ■ ⒦⒦⒦

This historic restaurant is in the city's
oldest building. The menu is gourmet
and the setting formal.

④ Geist
MAP K4 ■ Kongens Nytorv 8
■ 33 13 37 13 ■ www.restaurantgeist.
dk ■ ⒦⒦

Stylish eatery, both lavish and
informal; compose your meal from a
long list of small- and medium-sized
dishes, including vegetarian options.

⑤ Atlas Bar
MAP H4 ■ Larsbjørnsstræde 18
■ 33 15 03 52 ■ Closed Sun ■ www.
atlasbar.dk ■ ⒦⒦

Locals head to this cool basement
for a wide range of exotic dishes.

⑥ Krogs Fiskerestaurant
MAP J4 ■ Gammel Strand 38
■ 33 15 89 15 ■ Closed Sun D ■ www.
krogs.dk ■ ⒦⒦

This landmark fish restaurant offers
organic and sustainable lunch menus.

⑦ Bror
MAP H4 ■ Skt. Peders Stræde
24A ■ 32 17 59 99 ■ Open Wed–Sun D
■ www.restaurantbror.dk ■ ⒦⒦

This small restaurant offers
some innovative
Scandinavian dishes
from two former Noma
chefs (see p61).

⑧ Bankeråt
MAP G3 ■
Ahlefeldtsgade 29
■ 33 93 69 88 ■ www.
bankeraat.dk ■ ⒦⒦

Enjoy steaks, salads and
beers in this artistic venue

⑨ Restaurant Peder Oxe
MAP J4 ■ Gråbrødretov 11
■ 33 11 00 77 ■ Open 11:30am–11pm
daily ■ www.pederoxe.dk ■ ⒦⒦

A well established restaurant on a
picturesque square.

⑩ Kompasset
MAP L4 ■ Nyhavn 65 ■ 44 22
52 22 ■ www.restaurantkompasset.
dk ■ ⒦⒦

This restaurant has a smørrebrød
focus and is the perfect spot for
lunch overlooking the harbour.

Outdoor seating at Kompasset

🔟 Nørrebro, Østerbro and North of Gothersgade

Of these three neighbourhoods, two are additions to the original Copenhagen site, which took up what is now called the "Inner City". Until the 19th century, this area was mainly farmland; today it is a lively, multicultural part of the city with plenty of bars, cafés and alternative shopping centres. Østerbro, slightly northeast of Nørrebro, has remained an uncluttered, suburban residential area since the 19th century. The area north of Gothersgade is part of the Inner City and takes in later parts of the capital dating back to the Renaissance period.

Vase from the Designmuseum *(see p79)*

NØRREBRO, ØSTERBRO AND NORTH OF GOTHERSGADE

- **1** Top 10 Sights
  see pp77–9
- **1** Places to Eat
  see p83
- **1** Shops
  see p81
- **1** The Best of the Rest
  see p80
- **1** Nightlife
  see p82

1 Assistens Kirkegård

MAP C3 ■ Kapelvej ■ 35 37 19 17 ■ Open Apr–Sep: 7am–10pm daily; Oct–Mar: 7am–7pm daily ■ www.assistens.dk

If you are not a devoted fan of famous dead Danes, this cemetery may not be top of your list. However, it is a wonderful place to relax or take a romantic walk. The churchyard is beautiful and is located in the gritty Nørrebro district.

2 Marmorkirken

Standing close to Amalienborg is the splendid Marmorkirken or Marble Church (see pp24–5), a part of the great architectural design for the area of Frederiksstaden. However, plans for its construction were so

The splendid Marmorkirken cupola

extravagant that finances ran out and work was abandoned in 1770. For more than a century, it stood as a picturesque ruin before being rescued and financed by a Danish industrialist, and in 1894 the church was finally completed.

3 Amalienborg

If you wish to see inside the royal palaces, you need to visit on a summer weekend; otherwise you can only visit those areas that have been set up as a museum. The palaces were built as an important part of the 18th-century aristocratic district Frederiksstaden (see pp24–5) and are very different from the narrow streets and houses of the old quarter. When the complex was first built, it was visually linked to the Marble Church; the Opera House (see pp94–5) and the construction across the harbour on Holmen offer a contemporary visual contrast.

Amalienborg royal palace

The manicured gardens of Botanisk Have

4 Botanisk Have

MAP H2–J2 ▪ Gothersgade 128; Øster Farimagsgade 2C ▪ Open May–Sep: 8:30am–6pm daily; Oct–Apr: 8:30am–4pm daily ▪ www.botanik.snm.ku.dk

Among the prettiest outdoor spaces in Copenhagen, these gardens are studded with lakes, bridges and lovely flowerbeds (see p64). Climb the winding staircase for a great view of exotic trees below. The grounds are also home to three museums which cover botany, geology and zoology. By 2021, all three museums will be under one roof in the gardens.

5 Davids Samling

MAP K3 ▪ Kronprinsessegade 30–32 ▪ 33 73 49 49 ▪ Open 10am–5pm Tue–Sun (until 9pm Wed) ▪ www.davidmus.dk

This museum holds the private art collection of Danish Supreme Court barrister and art lover, C L David. The fine Islamic collection is Scandinavia's largest, and includes a fine range of Islamic art from the 8th to the 19th centuries. There is also a collection of 18th- and 19th-century European decorative arts. The collection is set in an elegant 19th-century town house.

Statue at Rosenborg Slot

6 Den Hirschsprungske Samling

MAP J1 ▪ Stockholmsgade 20 ▪ 35 42 03 36 ▪ Open 11am–4pm Wed–Sun ▪ Adm; free with Copenhagen Card ▪ www.hirschsprung.dk

This small art museum is situated just behind the National Gallery and displays the collection of tobacco magnate Heinrich Hirschsprung, given to the nation in 1902. Housed in a 19th-century building, the large collection is fittingly dedicated to 19th- and early 20th-century Danish art, including works by painters of the Golden Age and the North Jutland colony of Skagen painters, known for their bright colours and luminous treatment of light. Contemporary furniture is also displayed in the museum.

7 Rosenborg Slot and Kongens Have

Rosenborg Castle and the King's Garden are among the city's highlights (see p16–17), especially on sunny days when the park is full of people and entertainment. Rosenborg Slot was built in 1606–34 and is the only castle in the city centre that has not succumbed to fire. Little has changed about the structure since the time the royals inhabited it in the 17th century.

⑧ Frihedsmuseet
MAP L2 ∎ Churchill-parken 7
∎ 33 47 39 21 ∎ Closed until 2019
∎ www.natmus.dk

The Museum of Danish Resistance pays tribute to, and tells the stories of, the people who lived in Denmark during the German occupation (1940–45). It explores their resistance activities, from underground newspapers and radio stations to sabotage and the rescue of virtually every Jew in Denmark from under the noses of the Germans. The museum is closed due to fire damage and is likely to reopen at the end of 2019.

⑨ Statens Museum for Kunst
The National Gallery has a collection of both national and international art, including works by the Old Masters and modern icons (see pp26–7).

Art at the Statens Museum for Kunst

⑩ Designmuseum Danmark
MAP L2 ∎ Bredgade 68 ∎ 33 18 56 56 ∎ Open 11am–6pm Tue–Sun (until 9pm Wed) ∎ Adm; free with Copenhagen Card ∎ www.design museum.dk

Dedicated entirely to the art of design, this museum is housed in a splendid 18th-century Rococo building. The collection comprises everything from Danish-designed colanders and cardboard chairs to posters, textiles and Chinese decorative arts (see p44).

A WALK NORTH OF GOTHERSGADE

[Map showing walking route with labels: The Little Mermaid, Den Hirschsprungske Samling, Gefionspringvandet, Statens Museum for Kunst, Frihedsmuseet, Botanisk Have, Marmorkirken, Rosenborg Slot, Davids Samling, Amalienborg, Opera House]

▶ MORNING

Start your day at the **Den Hirschsprungske Samling** museum, among the Impressionistic paintings of the Danish Skagen colony of painters. Then cross the gardens to the impressive **Statens Museum for Kunst**; take an audio guide to learn about the displays.

AFTERNOON

For lunch, stop at either the museum café or the **Botanisk Have** café, depending upon the weather. The gardens are a great place for a picnic, too. Don't forget to visit the Palm House. Heading out from the gate on Øster Voldgade, cross over to **Rosenborg Slot**. You can spend a few enjoyable hours here, visiting the castle, the crown jewels and strolling through the gardens.

Afterwards leave from the Kronprinsessegade gate and pop into **Davids Samling** to see some Islamic art. Walk down Dronningens Tværgade, take a left onto Bredgade and walk right up to **Marmorkirken** (see p77). If you are here by 3pm, take a tour up the tower. Right in front of the church is **Amalienborg** (see p77). Take a walk through it to the pretty banks of the harbour and see the **Opera House** (see p94) across the water. If you are up for a 20-minute walk, head towards **The Little Mermaid** (see p80), passing **Gefionspringvandet** (see p80) and **Frihedsmuseet** (temporarily closed). To get back to town, hop onto the No. 26 bus from Folke Bernadottes Allé.

See map on pp76–7 ←

The Best of the Rest

1 ### Gefionspringvandet
MAP M2 ■ Langelinie

This bronze statue is a dramatic sight, representing the tale of the goddess Gefion as she ploughs enough land to create the island of Zealand, on which Copenhagen is found.

The bronze statue of goddess Gefion

2 ### Medicinsk Museion
MAP L2 ■ Bredgade 62 ■ 35 32 38 00 ■ Open noon–4pm Wed–Fri & Sun ■ Guided tour in English 2pm Wed–Fri, 1:30pm Sun ■ Adm ■ www. museion.ku.dk

The Medical Museum of Copenhagen University has exhibits dating back to the 18th century.

3 ### The Little Mermaid (Den Lille Havfrue)
MAP M1 ■ Langelinie, top of Kastellet

This statue of the heroine of Hans Christian Andersen's fairy tale, *The Little Mermaid*, perched on a rock in the harbour, has been staring out to sea since 1913 (see p13).

4 ### Amaliehaven
Filled with box hedges and fountains, this modern park lies to the east of Amalienborg, facing the harbour, with views of the Opera House (see p24).

5 ### Alexander Nevsky Kirke
MAP L3 ■ Bredgade 53 ■ 33 13 60 46 ■ Open 11:30am–1:30pm daily

This Russian Orthodox church (1883) was a gift from Tsar Alexander III to celebrate his marriage to the Danish Princess Marie Dagmar.

6 ### Kastelskirken
MAP L1 ■ Kastellet ■ 33 15 65 58 ■ Open 8am–6pm Mon–Fri

The military church at Kastellet has been holding services here since the 17th century.

7 ### St Alban's Church
MAP M2 ■ Churchillparken 11 ■ 33 11 85 18 ■ Open to visitors in summer, 10am–4pm Mon–Fri ■ www. st-albans.dk

St Alban's is Denmark's only Anglican church and is a Neo-Gothic building dating from 1885.

8 ### Kongelige Afstøbningssamling
MAP M2 ■ Toldbodgade 40 ■ 33 74 84 84 ■ Open for special events ■ www.smk.dk

The Royal Cast Collection is heralded on the harbour with a replica of Michelangelo's statue of *David*.

9 ### Fælledparken
MAP D2

Copenhagen's largest park is where the city gathers for the annual 1 May springtime celebrations (see p53).

10 ### Kastellet
MAP L1 ■ 33 47 95 00 ■ Only grounds open to visitors

This pentagram-shaped fortress was constructed as protection against the Swedes, but was only ever used against the English in 1807.

A cannon on show at Kastellet

Shops

1 Nyhavns Glaspusteri
MAP L4 ▪ Toldbodgade 4 ▪ 33 13 01 34 ▪ www.copenhagenglass.dk

This charming glass gallery is where glass-blower Christian Edwards sculpts and sells his creations.

2 Divaen og Krudtuglen
MAP C3 ▪ Elmegade 22 ▪ 26 71 59 68 ▪ www.millou.dk

Bright clothes and shoes for kids and mums alike, as well as trays of cute, inexpensive toys. Look out for the ecofriendly labelled brands.

3 Sneakers & Coffee
▪ Jægersborggade 30 ▪ Closed Sun

Indulge your sneaker craze at this hip shop stocking rare kicks such as retro Adidas and Finnish Karhus. The coffee bar keeps shoppers amped during fittings.

4 Tage Andersen Boutique & Museum
MAP K4 ▪ Ny Adelgade 12 ▪ 33 93 09 13 ▪ Adm ▪ www.tage-andersen.com

Run by flower artist and designer Tage Andersen, this flower shop, gallery and museum is full of lovely and unique arrangements. To see the whole place you'll need to climb up a steep staircase.

5 Eco Ego
MAP H3 ▪ Nørre Farimagsgade 82 ▪ 32 12 06 12 ▪ www.ecoego.dk

Denmark's first fair-trade, organic lifestyle shop sells everything from shoes and skincare products to games. There's a good selection of eco and ethical products for children.

6 Brund
MAP E2 ▪ Nordre Frihavnsgade 49 ▪ 35 43 51 33 ▪ www.brund.dk

Raw denim and bench-made boots line the shelves of this rugged menswear shop, which stocks a selection of high-end goods from brands including Loake, John Smedley and Crockett & Jones.

Interior of Normann Copenhagen

7 Normann Copenhagen
MAP E2 ▪ Østerbrogade 70 ▪ 35 27 05 40 ▪ www.normann-copenhagen.com

This vast warehouse housed in an old cinema sells designer furniture, clothes and interior design items.

8 Susanne Juul
MAP K3 ▪ Store Kongensgade 14 ▪ 33 32 25 22 ▪ Closed Sun & Mon ▪ www.susannejuul.dk

Suppliers of glamorous, ornate hats to royalty and celebrities.

9 Dag & Hammar
MAP E2 ▪ Nordre Frihavnsgade 19 ▪ 31 37 77 20

This smart men's boutique also stocks threads from the likes of Fred Perry and Amor Lux, as well as Clark's Originals shoes.

10 Mondo Kaos
MAP C3 ▪ Birkegade 1 ▪ 60 95 11 36 ▪ www.mondokaos.dk

New versions of vintage clothes, including retro 1950s-style dresses, are on the racks of this colourful rockabilly boutique.

See map on pp76–7 ←

Nightlife

1 BRUS
MAP C3 ■ Guldbergsgade 29 ■ 75 22 22 00 ■ www.tapperietbrus.dk
With 33 draft beers and an in-house bottleshop, there's plenty to keep even the thirstiest beer lover interested at this Nørrebro brewpub.

2 Gefährlich
MAP C3 ■ Fælledvej 7 ■ 35 24 13 24 ■ Closed Mon & Sun ■ www.gefahrlich.dk
This is one of the area's most popular bars. It also has a good restaurant and live music (see p57).

3 Bodega
MAP C3 ■ Kapelvej 1 ■ 35 39 07 07 ■ www.bodega.dk
This popular pre-clubbing venue serves good bar food. DJ sessions are held on Fridays and Saturdays.

4 The Barking Dog
MAP D3 ■ Sankt Hans Gade 19 ■ 35 36 16 00 ■ www.thebarkingdog.dk
This wallet-friendly cocktail bar is a hit with students and hipsters alike, where mixologists spin classic funk and soul records while they create weird and wonderful drinks.

5 Empire Bio Cinema
MAP C3 ■ Guldbergsgade 29F ■ 35 36 00 36 ■ www.empirebio.dk
This comfortable arts cinema holds good programmes and has a cosy bar and café area.

6 Søernes Ølbar
MAP E2 ■ Sortedam Dossering 83 ■ 32 19 63 80 ■ www.soernes oelbar.dk
A lakeside craft-beer joint with an impeccable selection of draft and bottled ales, porters and sours, this is a haven for hopheads on the hunt for rare and obscure brews.

7 DuPong
MAP C4 ■ Griffenfeldsgade 52 ■ 60 87 19 91 ■ www.dupong.dk
Cheap beer and table football make this cosy little bar a must-visit for pub sports enthusiasts.

8 The Oak Room
MAP C3 ■ Birkegade 10 ■ 38 60 38 60 ■ Open Wed–Sat ■ www.oakroom.dk
This cocktail bar consists of one long narrow room. Popular with locals.

9 Mexibar
MAP C3 ■ Elmegade 27 ■ 35 37 77 66 ■ Closed Sun
This cosy, Mexican-inspired bar serves good cocktails. The staff create a friendly atmosphere.

10 Rust
MAP C3 ■ Guldbergsgade 8 ■ 35 24 52 00 ■ Open 11pm–4am Wed, 8pm–5am Fri & Sat ■ www.rust.dk
Tune into Copenhagen's alternative live music scene at this bar (see p56).

The bar and booths at Rust

Places to Eat

① Orangeriet Kongens Have
MAP K3 ■ Kronprinsessegade 13
■ 33 11 13 07 ■ Close Sun D ■ www.
restaurant-orangeriet.dk ■ Ⓚ Ⓚ
This elegant orangery in the park
offers open sandwiches during the
day and light seasonal dishes in
the evening.

PRICE CATEGORIES
For a three-course meal for one without
alcohol, including taxes and charges.
....
Ⓚ under 300 Dkr Ⓚ Ⓚ 300–500 Dkr
Ⓚ Ⓚ Ⓚ over 500 Dkr

Interior of Orangeriet Kongens Have

② Ida Davidsen
MAP K3 ■ Store Kongensgade
70 ■ 33 91 36 55 ■ Open for lunch,
closed Sat–Sun & Jul ■ www.
idadavidsen.dk ■ Ⓚ Ⓚ
Excellent *smørrebrød* are on offer
here, with an array of toppings.

③ Restaurant Zeleste
MAP L4 ■ Store Strandstræde 6
■ 33 16 06 06 ■ www.zeleste.dk ■ Ⓚ Ⓚ
This charming restaurant with a cosy
interior serves elegantly executed
Danish dishes.

④ Kiin Kiin
MAP C3 ■ Guldbergsgade 21 ■
35 35 75 55 ■ Open 5:30pm–midnight
Mon–Sat ■ www.kiin.dk ■ Ⓚ Ⓚ Ⓚ
Here, Thai street food meets
inventive fusion cooking *(see p60)*.

⑤ Bæst
MAP C3 ■ Guldbergsgade 29
■ 35 35 04 63 ■ www.baest.dk ■ Ⓚ Ⓚ
This Italian diner sources ingredients
locally, and serves wood-fired pizzas.

⑥ Ramen To Biiru
MAP C3 ■ Griffenfeldsgade 28
■ 50 53 02 22 ■ www.
ramentobiiru.dk ■ Ⓚ
This quirky craft beer
and noodle bar oozes
authenticity, right down
to the retro-futuristic
vending machine where
you place your order.

⑦ Salt Bar and Restaurant
MAP L3 ■ Toldbodgade
24–8 ■ 33 74 14 44
■ www.saltrestaurant.dk
■ Ⓚ Ⓚ Ⓚ
In an airy 18th-century
granary, this elegant bar
and restaurant serves cocktails and
innovative French-Danish cuisine.

⑧ Relæ
Jægersborggade ■ 36 96 66 09
■ Open noon–1:30pm, 5pm–10pm
daily (closed lunch Fri & Sat) ■ www.
restaurant-relae.dk ■ Ⓚ Ⓚ Ⓚ Ⓚ
Savour Michelin-starred yet budget-
friendly New Nordic cuisine in a
laid-back environment *(see p60)*.

⑨ Fischer
MAP E2 ■ Victor Borges Plads
12 ■ 35 42 39 64 ■ Open 8am–3pm &
5:30pm–midnight Wed–Fri, 10am–
3pm & 5:30pm–midnight Sat & Sun
■ www.hosfischer.dk ■ Ⓚ Ⓚ
This tiny Italian restaurant is a
favourite with local restaurant critics.
Booking is essential.

⑩ Kate's Joint
MAP C4 ■ Blågårdsgade 12
■ 35 37 44 96 ■ Open D only ■ Ⓚ
Offers cheap dishes with South
American and Caribbean influences.

See map on pp76–7 ⬅

TOP10 Vesterbro and Frederiksberg

Vesterbro and Frederiksberg lie side by side to the southwest and west of the Inner City. In the 19th century both areas were outside the city walls; this was when Tivoli was built on Vesterbro's edge. Vesterbro formerly included a red-light district, and its poor lived in humble flats with no running water. Although the area retains an edginess shared only by the Nørrebro district, much of it has now been regenerated. Today, you will find a thriving underground culture, restaurants and bars, designer outlets and a multicultural population. In contrast, prosperous Frederiksberg is still a tranquil, upmarket residential area.

Flying Toucan

VESTERBRO AND FREDERIKSBERG

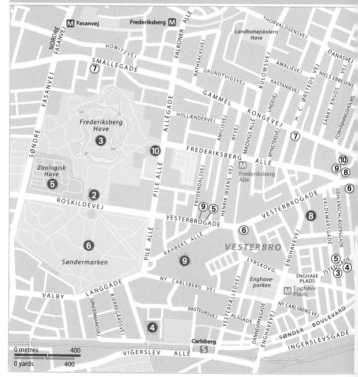

Previous pages The chapel at Frederiksberg Slot

Tycho Brahe Planetarium exterior

1 Tycho Brahe Planetarium

MAP C5 ▪ Gammel Kongevej 10 ▪ Open noon–7:40pm Mon, 9:30am–7:40pm Tue–Thu, 10:45am–8.50pm Fri & Sat, 10:45am–7:40pm Sun ▪ Adm; free with Copenhagen Card ▪ www.tycho.dk

The permanent exhibition at the planetarium includes displays on the natural sciences, astronomy and space travel. However, one of the biggest attractions is the IMAX cinema; visitors are blown away by the high-quality images on the enormous 1,000-sq-m (10,760-sq-ft) dome screen. Films cover topics like astronomy and space research, and virtually transport you to another world. The minimum age for films is 3 years.

2 Frederiksberg Slot

MAP A5 ▪ Roskildevej 28A ▪ 72 81 77 71

Set in Frederiksberg Have, one of the most romantic spots in Copenhagen, this Baroque-style palace was the royal family's summer residence until the mid-1800s. It's perched on a park hilltop, surrounded by many lovely little bridges, and the Chinese Pavilion that was erected in 1799 as a royal teahouse. It now houses the Danish Officer's Academy and is only open for guided tours.

3 Frederiksberg Have

MAP A5 ▪ Frederiksberg Runddel ▪ 33 95 42 00 ▪ Open 7am–sunset daily

Surrounding Frederiksberg Slot, this park makes up one of the city's loveliest green areas. Between 1798 and 1802, the original Baroque gardens were landscaped to conform with the Romantic style of the English garden. Several buildings here date to the Golden Age (1800–50), including the Chinese Pavilion and the Apis Temple.

Frederiksberg Have in the summer

1 **Top 10 Sights**
see pp87–9

1 **Places to Eat**
see p91

1 **Shopping**
see p90

4 Carlsberg Brewery

MAP A6 ■ Gamle Carlsberg Vej 11 ■ 33 27 10 20 ■ Open 10am–5pm daily ■ Adm (free for under-6s); free with Copenhagen Card ■ www.visitcarlsberg.dk

The Carlsberg Brewery offers an exhibition and tour charting the brewery's history and its brands (including a collection of over 16,000 beer bottles). Carlsberg is no longer produced on the premises (only Jacobsen Brewery survives), but the rich history of brewing can still be discovered here. Other parts of the brewery have been developed into a cultural quarter, Carlsberg Byen, with art galleries, an adventure park and the Fotografisk Center.

5 Zoologisk Have

MAP A5 ■ Roskildevej 32 ■ 72 20 02 00 ■ Open Apr–May & Sep: 10am–5pm Mon–Fri, 10am–6pm Sat–Sun; Jun & last 2 weeks of Aug: 10am–6pm daily; Jul & first 2 weeks of Aug: 10am–8pm daily; Oct– Mar: 10am–4pm daily (until 5pm Oct) ■ Adm; free with Copenhagen Card ■ www.zoo.dk

Open 365 days a year, this zoo makes for a lovely day out. Here you will find a wide variety of animals, from tigers to monkeys (including tiny, endangered Golden Lion Tamarins). Make sure you visit the Arctic Ring exhibit, which gives you a unique opportunity to get closer to the magnificent polar bears, North Atlantic birds and seals.

Interior of the Cisternerne

6 Cisternerne – The Cisterns

MAP A6 ■ Søndermarken 25 ■ 33 21 93 10 ■ Open 11am–5pm Tue–Sun ■ Closed Dec–Feb ■ Adm; free for under-18s ■ www.cisternerne.dk

This candlelit glass space features exhibits by artists like Per Kirkeby and Robert Jacobsen. Set inside the cave-like water cistern of an old supply plant, it lies beneath the lawns of Frederiksberg Have and has thin stalactites on the ceiling.

7 Radisson Blu Royal Hotel

This 20-storey tower-block hotel, designed by architect Arne Jacobsen, represents the cutting-edge design of the 1950s, and is littered with his iconic Egg and Swan chairs (see p116).

A tiger relaxes in the snow at Zoologisk Have

8 WestMarket
MAP C5 ▪ Vesterbrogade 97
▪ 70 50 00 05 ▪ Open 8am–10pm
daily ▪ www.westmarket.dk

A huge indoor street-food market in
the heart of vibrant Vesterbro, this is
the perfect place to grab a bite to eat
while on the go. A meal certainly
won't break the bank, and the range
of food on offer is superb, with stalls
selling everything from Vietnamese
bao to Jamaican jerk chicken. For
those preferring to cook at home,
there are also several delicatessens
selling fresh produce, as well as
specialist wine and beer shops.

9 Bakkehusmuseet
MAP B6 ▪ Rahbeks Allé 23,
Frederiksberg ▪ 33 31 43 62 ▪ Open
11am–4pm Tue–Sun ▪ Adm ▪ www.
bakkehusmuseet.dk

Formerly the home of 19th-century
Golden Age literary personalities
Knud Lyne and Kamma Rahbek, this
old house is now a cultural museum.

A room at Bakkehusmuseet

10 Storm P Museet
MAP A5 ▪ Frederiksberg
Runddel ▪ 38 86 05 00 ▪ Open
10am–4pm Tue–Sun ▪ Adm; free with
Copenhagen Card ▪ www.stormp.dk

This small museum is a delightful
find. It is dedicated to the whimsical
and satirical wit of the Danish car-
toonist Storm P, whose distinctive
style seems to recall the social
realism of the late 19th and early
20th centuries, such as the styles
of Daumier and Degas. His great
sense of humour comes through in
the dialogues of his characters. If you
speak Danish, you will derive great
enjoyment from these cartoons.

A WALK AROUND VESTERBRO

▶ MORNING

Start at the city's central station,
Hovedbanegård, and admire the
Frihedsstøtten or "pillar of freedom" (1792). Continue down
Vesterbrogade and take a left at
Reverdilsgade, then take a
right onto Istedgade. Walk up to
Halmtorvet, a former cattle
market now full of cafés, known
as Den Brune Kødby ("brown
meat city"). The building opposite
is Øksnehallen, Vesterbro's biggest cultural exhibition space.
Stroll to the blue-painted
complex, Den Hvide Kødby
("white meat city"), now a lively
cluster of bars and galleries. Head
back to Halmtorvet, walk on and
take a right on Skydebanegade.
At the end of the street is a wall
that protected inhabitants from
shooting practice in the gardens
on the other side. Enter the gate
in the wall, turn left and walk
through the park on your right
to Vesterbrogade. Turn left and
walk down the street, taking a
left onto Oehlenschlægersgade,
where you will find an extraordinary mosaic-covered building
created by the late Nigerian-born
artist Manuel Tafat.

AFTERNOON

Head back to Vesterbrogade
for lunch at Les Trois Cochons
(see p91), or continue down
Oehlenschlægersgade until you
reach the trendy bars and boutiques on Istedgade. You could
also stop for lunch or a drink at
Café Bang & Jensen (see p91).
Spend the rest of the afternoon
browsing in the stylish shops.

See map on pp86–7

Shopping

Bold furnishings and accessories on display at Danefæ

1 Danefæ
MAP C6 ▪ Istedgade 83 ▪ 61 30 84 85 ▪ www.danefae.dk

This popular Danish clothing brand opened its Vesterbro branch in 2013. It specializes in quirky, brightly coloured separates with bold motifs.

2 Donn Ya Doll
MAP C5 ▪ Istedgade 55 ▪ 33 22 66 35

Donn Ya Doll opened in the 1990s and has something of a space-age look. It stocks original accessories and clothing, some designed by the owner.

3 Girlie Hurly
MAP C6 ▪ Istedgade 99 ▪ 33 24 22 41

This shop is filled with quirky, colourful items for girls, from bags and candles to lamps and crockery.

4 Rockahula
MAP C6 ▪ Istedgade 91 ▪ 26 23 42 67 ▪ www.rockahula.dk

This intriguing little boutique is dedicated to all things 1950s and rockabilly, including a children's line.

5 Klaus Samsøe
MAP B5 ▪ Vesterbrogade 178 ▪ www.samsoe.com

With meat hooks in the ceiling, this bright and airy store is the offbeat brother of menswear designer Samsøe's city branches.

6 Designer Zoo
MAP B5 ▪ Vesterbrogade 137 ▪ 33 24 94 93 ▪ www.dzoo.dk

This is a mecca for the design conscious, with clothing, ceramics, jewellery and even furniture by in-house designers.

7 Meyers Deli
MAP B5 ▪ Gammel Kongevej 107 ▪ 33 25 45 95 ▪ Open until 8pm daily ▪ www.meyersdeli.dk

Claus Meyer helped kickstart the Nordic kitchen movement and his deli provides Noma-style food, from relishes to ready meals.

8 Dora
MAP C5 ▪ Værnedamsvej 6 ▪ 32 21 33 57 ▪ www.shopdora.dk

Stylish and playful homewares, beautiful jewellery, fun stationery and more; all with reasonable price tags.

9 Værnedamsvej
MAP C5

This gourmet food street has wine and chocolate shops, butchers and fishmongers among other stores.

10 DANSK Made for Rooms
MAP C5 ▪ Istedgade 80 ▪ 32 18 02 55 ▪ www.danskmadeforrooms.dk

An enclave of slick Danish design, from prints and kitchen appliances to decor. Great for window-shopping on Vesterbo's vibrant high street.

Places to Eat

PRICE CATEGORIES

For a three-course meal for one without alcohol, including taxes and charges.

Ⓚ under 300 Dkr ⒦ⓚ 300–500 Dkr
ⓚⓚⓚ over 500 Dkr

1 Gorilla
MAP D6 ▪ Flæsketorvet 63
▪ 33 33 83 30 ▪ Open 5:30pm–midnight Mon–Thu; 5:30pm–2am Fri & Sat
▪ www.restaurantgorilla.dk ▪ ⓚⓚ
Tuck into shared plates of sumptuous Scandi-tapas while slurping biodynamic wines at this trendy brasserie-style restaurant in Kødbyen.

2 Sticks 'n' Sushi
MAP C6 ▪ Istedgade 62
▪ 33 23 73 04 ▪ www.sushi.dk ▪ ⓚⓚ
Try mouthwatering sushi, sashimi or yakitori at this Euro-Japanese café-bar.

3 Kul
MAP C5 ▪ Høkerboderne 16b
▪ 33 21 00 33 ▪ Open noon–3pm & 6–10pm daily (until 11pm Thu–Sun)
▪ www.restaurantkul.dk ▪ ⓚⓚⓚ
This uber-hip restaurant in the meat-packing district has its own custom-built grill and a knack for pulling off unlikely food pairings (see p61).

4 Cofoco
MAP C5 ▪ Abel Cathrines Gade 7 ▪ 33 13 60 60 ▪ Book ahead ▪ ⓚ
Delicious and reasonably priced Mediterranean-Danish food is served at a long communal table.

5 Café Bang & Jensen
MAP C6 ▪ Istedgade 130
▪ 33 25 53 18 ▪ www.bangogjensen.dk ▪ ⓚ
This former pharmacy is now a popular café-bar. Fun cocktails and good music make for lively nights.

6 Famo
MAP C5 ▪ Saxogade 3 ▪ 33 23 22 50 ▪ www.famo.dk ▪ ⓚⓚ
Locals head here for good-quality, inexpensive Italian cuisine.

7 Frederiks Have
MAP A4 ▪ Smallegade 41
▪ 38 88 33 35 ▪ Closed Sun ▪ www.frederikshave.dk ▪ ⓚⓚ
Housed in a 19th-century building, Frederiks Have serves Swedish and Danish specialities.

8 Mother
MAP C6 ▪ Høkerboderne 9–15 ▪ 22 27 58 98 ▪ www.mother.dk ▪ ⓚ
This hip pizzeria is known for sourdough bases and fresh, classic toppings.

Sushi plate at Sticks 'n' Sushi

9 Formel B
MAP B5 ▪ Vesterbrogade 182 ▪ 33 25 10 66 ▪ Closed Sun ▪ www.formelb.dk ▪ ⓚⓚⓚ
Enjoy delicate small plates made with farm-fresh ingredients. Known for a selection of natural wines (see p60).

10 Les Trois Cochons
MAP C5 ▪ Værnedamsvej 10
▪ 33 31 70 55 ▪ ⓚⓚ
Aptly named ("the three pigs" in French), this restaurant serves great southern French food.

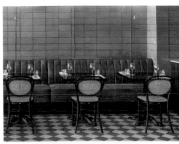

Dining booths at Les Trois Cochons

See map on pp86–7

TOP 10 Christianshavn and Holmen

After the Inner City, this settlement on the island of Amager is the oldest part of Copenhagen. In 1521, Christian II invited Dutch gardeners (whom he held in high regard) to this fertile area to plant and run market gardens. A century later, Christian IV built fortifications in the area and a town on an island at the north end. The canals of Christianshavn, lined with houseboats and pretty 17th-century houses, are a charming attraction. Holmen to the north consists of three man-made islets and was created in 1690 as a naval base. After the navy left in the late 20th century, the area saw an increase in public spaces, housing and art and design schools; it is also home to the city's impressive Opera House.

CHRISTIANSHAVN AND HOLMEN

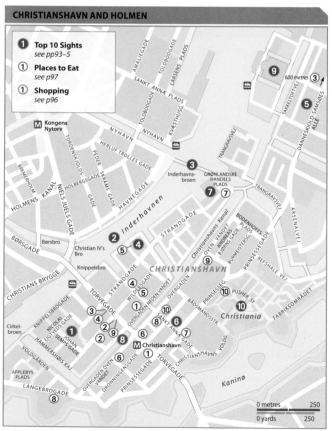

Inderhavnsbroen bridge

1 Christians Kirke
**MAP K6 ■ Strandgade 1 ■ 32
54 15 76 ■ Open 9am–4pm Tue–Fri
■ www.christianskirke.com**

Originally known as Frederiks Kirke,
this yellow-brick church was renamed
Christians Kirke (after Christian IV,
founder of this part of Copenhagen) in
1901. It was built between 1755 and
1759 in the Rococo style by Nicolai
Eigtved, Frederik V's master architect.
The interior resembles a theatre, with
second-level seating galleries and the
altar taking the place of the stage.
The elegant tower was added by
Eigtved's son-in-law, G D Anthon,
10 years after the church was built.

2 Inderhavnen
MAP J6–M4

Christianshavn is dominated by
waterways. Its canals are tributaries
of the Inner Harbour (Inderhavnen),
which separates it from the rest of the
city, eventually widening to become
the Øresund (Sound). A harbour tour
is a great way to
appreciate the area.

**Sailing boats at
Gammel Dok**

3 Harbour Circle
MAP K6–L5

Completed in 2017, the Harbour
Circle route is part of Copenhagen's
push for sustainable urban transport. The scenic pedestrian and
cyclist path connects previously
disjointed neighbourhoods along
the city harbour, from Holmen and
Nyhavn in the north to Christianshavn
and southernmost Slusen. The route
is connected by architecturally
noteworthy bridges. Inderhavnsbroen
(built 2016), nicknamed "The Kissing
Bridge", connects Nyhavn and the
city centre with Christianshavn and
Holmen. Platforms on the bridge
offer spectacular views of the harbour
area. Danish-Icelandic architect
Olafur Eliasson designed the striking
Cirkelbroen (The Circle Bridge): five
touching circular platforms with ship
masts link central Christianshavn to
Appelbys Plads.

4 Gammel Dok
**MAP L5 ■ Dansk Arkitektur
Centre, Strandgade 27B ■ 32 57
19 30 ■ Open 10am–5pm (until 9pm
Wed) ■ Adm; free 5–9pm; free with
Copenhagen Card ■ www.dac.dk**

Gammel Dok ("Old Dock") was built
in 1739, a time when the navy's ships
moored in the local area. The warehouse dates back to 1882 and is now
home to the Danish Architecture
Centre. It holds exhibitions and provides a working space for young
artists and architects to study here.
A café on the first floor offers great
views over the water.

⑤ Holmen and Refshaleøen

MAP M4

North of Christianshavn are Holmen and Refshaleøen, a former shipyard that is home to various sporting activities and is now a major dining destination. Innovative restaurants here include Noma *(see p97)*, and you will also find a new version of the Copenhagen Street Food Market.

North Atlantic House, a former warehouse

⑥ Vor Frelsers Kirke

MAP L6 ■ Sankt Annae Gade 29 ■ 32 54 68 83 ■ open 11am–3:30pm daily ■ Tower: Open Mar–May & Oct–Nov: 10am–4pm Mon–Sat, 10:30am–4pm Sun; Jun–Sep: 10am–7:30pm Mon–Sat, 10:30am–7:30pm Sun ■ Adm for tower; free with Copenhagen Card ■ www.vorfrelserskirke.dk

This magnificent Baroque church was built in 1682–96 by the Dutch-Norwegian architect Lambert van Haven in the form of a Greek cross. Its trademark twisted tower was added 50 years later. Inside the church, keep an eye out for the putti-covered font, presented in 1702 by Frederik IV's morganatic wife. Don't miss the altarpiece, which represents God as the Sun and depicts the scene in the garden of Gethsemane.

⑦ North Atlantic House

MAP M4 ■ Strandgade 91 ■ 32 83 37 00 ■ Open 10am–5pm Mon–Fri, noon–5pm Sat & Sun ■ Adm; free for under-11s and with Copenhagen Card ■ www.nordatlantens.dk

The North Atlantic House is a cultural centre for Greenland, Iceland and the Faroes. It is housed in an 18th-century warehouse, formerly the Greenlandic Trading Square, which hosts art displays and events.

⑧ Overgaden Neden Vandet and Overgaden Oven Vandet

MAP L6–M5

These two cobbled streets lie on either side of the Christianshavns canal. Overgaden Neden Vandet ("upper street below the water") is the quayside that runs along the Sound side of the canal. It is lined with 17th-century buildings, one of which is the Era Ora restaurant *(see p97)*. Overgaden Oven Vandet ("upper street above the water") is also lined with 17th-century houses.

⑨ Operaen

MAP M3 ■ Ekvipagemestervej 10 ■ 33 69 69 69 ■ Guided tours available ■ www.kglteater.dk

Completed in 2004, the Opera House was the first major public building to be built in the Holmen area after the navy vacated the docks. Architect Henning Larsen emphasized its location near the water, creating a

The twisted tower of Vor Frelsers

building with large glass windows and no pillars on the ground floor so as not to obstruct the view. The interior was designed to have a maritime feel as well, with big balconies, open spaces and white railings. The position of the Opera House caused major controversy when it was built, as it lies directly opposite Amalienborg. The design of the Opera House was also the cause of some friction when its benefactor, Mærsk McKinney Møller, insisted that his own ideas be incorporated into the construction. It is one of the most expensive opera houses ever built, thanks to its marble foyer and gold-leaf auditorium ceiling.

Modern interior of Operaen

10 Christiania
MAP M5

This rebellious squatters' enclave, set up in the 1970s in abandoned military barracks, was an inspirational new society with its own set of laws, readily available drugs and no tax system. The area has now become a bit more conventional; the inhabitants have been paying taxes since 1994, and the stands that sold drugs on Pusher Street closed down in 2004. In 2011, residents and the state came to an agreement giving Christiania residents the right to buy, making the squat official for the first time. There are no actual sights but many hippy hangouts (see pp28–9).

A WALKING TOUR OF THE AREA

▶ MORNING

Start at the **Knippelsbro** bridge. Built in 1937, the bridge takes its name from Hans Knip, the tollkeeper. Turn right to visit **Christians Kirke** (see p41) on Strandgade. Head north on Johan Semps Gade to catch a glimpse of Den Sorte Diamant library (see p12) across the harbour, then head west to cross **Cirkelbroen** (see p93), a pedestrian and bike bridge. Follow the path past Appelbys Plads to Overgaden Oven Vandet. Take a left and walk along the canal. Stop at **No. 32** (built 1622–4), on Strandgade, which is said to be the oldest house in Christianshavn. From here, turn right onto Sankt Annæ Gade to see **Vor Frelsers Kirke**. If you are curious about **Christiania**, follow Overgaden Oven Vandet until you can take a right down Brobergsgade, passing through the gate reading "You are now leaving the EU." Alternatively, stroll canalside and go right at Bodenhoffs Plads, then left onto Værftsbroen. Keep wal towards the **Opera House**. on a harbour bus back to Knippelsbro for lunch a **Wilder** (see p97) on W

AFTERNOON

Spend the after you are in the there are ca Christians over sup (Strand catch Hou ha

Shopping

 Bit Antik
MAP L6 ■ Prinsessegade 17B
■ 40 72 09 62 ■ Open 3–6pm Wed
■ www.bitantik.dk

This tiny shop is filled with pieces from Denmark's yesteryears, including old dolls and doll houses, books, glasses, sculpture and porcelain objects.

② Aurum
MAP L6 ■ Wildersgade 26
■ 25 30 00 11 ■ www.aurumcph.com

Some 20 international jewellers, including Marco Vallejo, are represented at Aurum. Many materials, including precious stones, are used to create these unique pieces.

Gold ring by Marco Vallejo

③ Porte à Gauche
MAP L5 ■ Torvegade 20 ■ 32 54 01 40 ■ www.porteagauche.dk

This trendy boutique offers chic, minimalist Scandinavian designer wear for women. You will also find a classic, exotic collection of Julie Sandlau jewellery.

④ Mo Christianshavn
MAP L5 ■ Torvegade 24
■ 26 80 17 70 ■ Open Thu–Sat
■ www.mo.dk

This small shop and workshop is owned by Mo, a popular jewellery designer.

Danish Architecture Shop
...dgade
...

...our

⑥ Lagkagehuset
MAP L6 ■ Torvegade 45
■ 32 57 36 07 ■ Open from 6am daily

Well known for its breads, cakes and pastries, this bakery has a fine selection during Christmas.

⑦ Pang Christianshavn
MAP L6 ■ Sankt Annæ Gade 31
■ 32 96 68 80 ■ www.pangchristianshavn.dk

This shop sells gifts, clothes and shoes, as well as all kinds of kitschy items for the home.

⑧ Hilbert København
MAP L6 ■ Sankt Annæ Gade 24 ■ 33 93 53 01
■ Closed Sat

Jewellery is made to order here by goldsmith Morten Hilbert.

⑨ Cibi e Vini
MAP L5 ■ Torvegade 28
■ 32 57 77 98 ■ www.cibievini.dk

This Italian delicatessen sells wine, bread, pasta and meats.

⑩ Christiania Shop
MAP M5 ■ Loppebygningen
■ 60 80 88 62

Located in the same building as the Christiania art gallery, this shop sells many Christiania souvenirs.

Mannequins outside Christiania Shop

Places to Eat

> **PRICE CATEGORIES**
>
> For a three-course meal for one without alcohol, including taxes and charges.
> ....
>
> ⓚ under 300 Dkr ⓚⓚ 300–500 Dkr
> ⓚⓚⓚ over 500 Dkr

① Era Ora
MAP L6 ■ Overgaden Neden Vandet 33B ■ 32 54 06 93 ■ Closed Sun ■ www. era-ora.dk ■ ⓚ ⓚ ⓚ
One of the best Italian restaurants in Denmark, Era Ora offers warm service in a tranquil setting, delicious food and a vast wine list (see p60). Book ahead.

② Kadeau
MAP L6 ■ Wildersgade 10B ■ 33 25 22 23 ■ Closed Sun–Tue, L ■ www.kadeau.dk ■ ⓚ ⓚ ⓚ
This Michelin-starred New Nordic restaurant's menu reads like a love letter to the island of Bornholm, from where all of the seasonal ingredients are painstakingly sourced (see p60).

③ Noma
Refshalevej 96 ■ 32 96 32 97 ■ Closed Sun–Tue ■ www.noma.dk ■ ⓚ ⓚ ⓚ
Copenhagen's ultimate Michelin-star restaurant reopened on Refshaleøen in 2018. The restaurant serves a New Nordic tasting menu from three seasonal themes: seafood, vegetables, and game and forest. Book ahead.

④ Luna's Diner
MAP L5 ■ Sankt Annæ Gade 5 ■ 32 54 20 00 ■ www.lunasdiner.dk ■ ⓚ ⓚ
Popular American-style diner in the heart of Christianshavn known for its burgers, breakfasts and vegetarian options.

⑤ Café Wilder
MAP L5 ■ Wildersgade 56 ■ 32 54 71 83 ■ www.cafewilder.dk ■ ⓚ ⓚ
Locals and tourists come here to enjoy good French- and Italian-inspired food and coffee.

⑥ Sofiekælderen
MAP L6 ■ Overgaden Oven Vandet 32 ■ 32 57 77 01 ■ Closed Sun ■ www.sofiekaelderen.dk ■ ⓚ ⓚ ⓚ
This café-bar is so close to the water, you could climb down to the boats moored alongside.

⑦ 108
MAP M4 ■ Strandgade 108 ■ 32 96 32 92 ■ www.108.dk ■ ⓚ ⓚ ⓚ
The sister to Noma, this harbourside bistro offers a masterclass in New Nordic cooking – and a fascinating selection of biodynamic wines.

Chic dining setting at 108

⑧ Rabes Have
MAP K6 ■ Langebrogade 8 ■ 32 57 34 17 ■ Open until 5pm ■ Closed Mon–Tue ■ ⓚ
Opened for soldiers and sailors in 1632, this is the oldest pub in the city.

⑨ Parterre
MAP M5 ■ Overgaden Oven Vandet 90 ■ ⓚ
A gorgeous, hidden-gem baseme[nt] café on Christianshavn's canal, [is] popular for breakfast and lunc[h].

⑩ Oven Vande Café
MAP L5 ■ Overgaden [Oven] Vandet 44 ■ 32 95 96 02 ■ [www.] cafeovenvande.dk ■ ⓚ ⓚ
Enjoy tasty salads, soups [...] at this café with outdoor [...]

🔟 Beyond Copenhagen

Although Copenhagen itself will easily keep you entertained for days, the area around the city offers many excursion options. Roskilde and Helsingør provide a taste of Nordic history, from the Viking era to the founding of Copenhagen. Get a sense of medieval maritime defence of the Sound at Helsingør's Kronborg Slot or explore royal lifestyles of the 17th and 18th centuries at Frederiksborg and Charlottenlund. Art- and literature-lovers will enjoy Arken, Louisiana, Ordrupgaard and the Karen Blixen Museet. Frilandsmuseet and Den Blå Planet are must-visits for kids.

Windmill at Frilandsmuseet

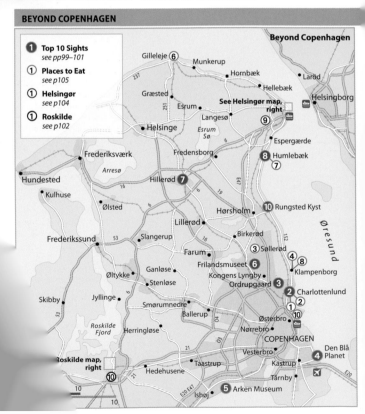

BEYOND COPENHAGEN

1 Top 10 Sights
see pp99–101

① Places to Eat
see p105

① Helsingør
see p104

① Roskilde
see p102

Beyond Copenhagen

Gilleleje **6**   Munkerup
            Hornbæk   Larød
237   Hellebæk
Græsted   **See Helsingør map,**   Helsingborg
            right
251 Esrum   Langesø   **9**
  • Helsinge   Esrum
              Sø   Espergærde
Frederiksværk   Fredensborg   **8** Humlebæk
   Arresø   **7**
Hundested   Hillerød **7**
  Kulhuse   19
        Ølsted   Hørsholm   **10** Rungsted Kyst
            Lillerød
Frederikssund 53 Slangerup   • Birkerød
              Farum   152   **3** Søllerød
        Ganløse   Frilandsmuseet **6**   **4** **8**
  Øltykke   Stenløse Kongens Lyngby   Klampenborg
Skibby Jyllinge   Ordrupgaard **3**   **2** Charlottenlund
   53   Smørumnedre   **1** **2**
        Ballerup   Østerbro   **10**
Roskilde
Fjord   Herringløse   Nørrebro
            21   Vesterbro COPENHAGEN
Roskilde map,   Den Blå
right   **4** Planet
   10   Hedehusene • Taastrup   Kastrup
10   Tårnby
   10   **5** Arken Museum
                    Ishøj •

Replica Viking longboats on the water in Roskilde

① Roskilde

The town of Roskilde makes for a fascinating day out. You will find a medieval cathedral, a royal burial site and the wonderful Viking Ship Museum, which offers fjord trips on replica Viking longboats *(see p102).*

② Charlottenlund Slotshave

MAP B2 ■ Open daily ■ www.slke.dk

The park around Charlottenlund Slot is a 16-minute train ride from the city centre. Redesigned in the Romantic English style in the 19th century, the park includes a charming thatched cottage, once lodgings for the Royal Life Guards. The palace itself is closed to the public.

③ Ordrupgaard

MAP B2 ■ Vilvordevej 110, Charlottenlund ■ 39 64 11 83 ■ Gallery open: 1–5pm Tue–Fri; Finn Juhl's House: 11am–4:45pm Sat, Sun & public holidays ■ Adm; free for under-18s; free with Copenhagen Card ■ Free audio guide; book for English guided tours ■ www.ordrupgaard.dk

This gallery houses a superb collection of French Impressionist art and works by 19th- and 20th-century Danish artists. The building is a 19th-century mansion with a modern extension by the late architect Zaha Hadid. Within the same complex is furniture designer Finn Juhl's house, now a gallery exhibiting his work.

The interior of Finn Juhl's house

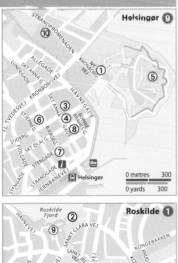

Marine life at Den Blå Planet

4 Den Blå Planet

MAP C3 ■ Jacob Fortlingsvej 1, Kastrup ■ 44 22 22 44 ■ Open 10am–5pm daily (until 9pm Mon) ■ Adm; free with Copenhagen Card ■ www. denblaaplanet.dk

Denmark's national aquarium has garnered much attention for its architecture, a spiralling vortex inspired by the currents of a whirlpool. Inside there are 53 aquariums in different habitats and over 20,000 marine animals.

5 Arken Museum for Moderne Kunst

MAP B3 ■ Skovvej 100, Ishøj ■ 43 54 02 22; Special tours: 43 57 34 55 ■ Open 10am–5pm Tue–Sun (until 9pm Wed) ■ Adm; free with Copenhagen Card ■ www.arken.dk

This wonderful museum houses a rotating permanent collection of contemporary international and Danish art, along with temporary exhibitions. The white, ship-like museum building, designed by Danish architect Søren Lund, could be an exhibit in itself. It offers great views of the sea at Køge Bugt.

6 Frilandsmuseet

MAP B2 ■ Konggevejen 100, Kongens Lyngby ■ 41 20 64 55 ■ Open May–mid-Oct: 10am–4pm Tue–Sun (Jul & first 2 wks of Aug: until 5pm) ■ en.natmus.dk

Part of the Nationalmuseet (see pp30–31), Denmark's Open Air Museum brings history alive through working exhibits from the period 1650–1940. Explore farms, windmills and a cooperative village. There are old Danish breeds of livestock, including pigs, sheep and geese.

7 Frederiksborg Slot

MAP B2 ■ DK-3400 Hillerød ■ 48 26 04 39 ■ Museum: open Apr–Oct: 10am–5pm daily; Nov–Mar: 11am–3pm ■ Baroque gardens: open 10am–sundown daily ■ Adm (museum only) ■ www.dnm.dk

This copper-turreted castle stands next to a lake and is surrounded by Baroque gardens (see p42). It was built in 1602–20 for Christian IV. The interior is a mix of Renaissance and Rococo decor. After a fire in 1859, the castle was rescued from ruin by J C Jacobsen (of Carlsberg fame), who founded a museum here.

The Great Hall at Frederiksborg Slot

⑧ Louisiana Museum
MAP B1 ▪ Gammel Strandvej 13, Humlebæk ▪ 49 19 07 19 ▪ Open 11am–10pm Tue–Fri, 11am–6pm Sat & Sun ▪ Adm for adults; free with Copenhagen Card ▪ English guided tours available ▪ www.louisiana.dk

This museum (see p103) houses an impressive selection of works by international artists like Picasso and Francis Bacon, and Danish masters including Asger Jorn and Per Kirkeby. There is also a children's wing, which offers art-related activities for kids aged between 3 and 16 years. The coastal location, sculpture park and excellent café make the museum even more appealing for visitors.

Courtyard at Kronborg Slot

⑨ Helsingør
In the 1400s, this harbour town levied tax on all sea traffic that passed through the Sound. A pretty medieval centre aside, there is the 16th-century castle, Kronborg Slot, the Carmelite monastery and the Maritime Museum of Denmark (see p104).

⑩ Karen Blixen Museet
MAP B2 ▪ Rungsted Strandvej 111, Rungsted Kyst ▪ 45 57 10 57 ▪ Open May–Sep: 10am–5pm Tue–Sun; Oct–Apr: 1–4pm Wed–Fri, 11am–4pm Sat & Sun ▪ Adm; free for under-14s; free with Copenhagen Card ▪ Book ahead for guided tours in English ▪ www.blixen.dk

Karen Blixen (pen name: Isak Dinesen), the author of the acclaimed memoir Out of Africa, was born here in 1885. Blixen returned in 1931 and the house is exactly as it was when she lived here.

DAY TOUR BEYOND COPENHAGEN

[map showing: Helsingør, Humlebæk, Rungsted Kyst, Klampenborg, Copenhagen Central Station]

▶ MORNING

Take a train from Københavns Hovedbanegård (Copenhagen Central Station) and head to the town of **Helsingør** to explore the local museums and castles. Have a wander around **Kronborg Slot** (see p104), a lovely 16th-century castle with a banqueting hall, royal chambers and casemates, and see why it was immortalized as Elsinore in Hamlet. After your castle tour, stop by the **Maritime Museum of Denmark** (see p104). For lunch, return to the town square and sit down for an open sandwich and a beer at one of its numerous pubs. After lunch, wander through the medieval streets, especially Stendgade and Strandgade (see p104). Visit the medieval **Domkirke** and the **Bymuseum** (see p104), housed in a small Carmelite hospital dating back to 1520.

AFTERNOON

Take the train to Humlebæk and visit the **Louisiana Museum** (see p103), which stays open until 10pm on Tuesdays to Fridays. There are plenty of things to see here, and you can book into a guided tour that encompasses the museum's architecture and landscape. Then return to the station and take a train to Rungsted Kyst and drop in at the Karen Blixen Museet. After a walk around the house, garden and bird sanctuary, enjoy coffee and one of the home-made cakes at the museum café. Head back towards Copenhagen in the early evening, stopping off en route at Klampenborg for dinner and an evening of entertainment at the **Bakken** funfair (see p52).

See map on p98 ←

Roskilde

(1) Roskilde Domkirke
MAP P6 ▪ Domkirkestræde 10
▪ 46 35 16 24 ▪ Open Apr–Sep: 10am–6pm daily (from 1pm Sun); Oct–Mar: 10am–4pm daily (from 1pm Sun)
▪ Adm; free with Copenhagen Card
▪ www.roskildedomkirke.dk

This magnificent cathedral holds the remains of 39 Danish monarchs.

Replica Viking vessels

(2) Vikingeskibsmuseet
MAP P4 ▪ Vindeboder 12 ▪ 46 30 02 00 ▪ Open 10am–4pm daily (to 5pm Jul–Aug) ▪ Adm; free for under-18s ▪ www.vikingeskibsmuseet.dk

The popular Viking Ship Museum displays five 1,000-year-old Viking vessels. Boat trips available May–Sep.

(3) Roskilde Museum
MAP P5 ▪ Sankt Ols Stræde 3
▪ 46 31 65 29 ▪ Open 11am–4pm daily ▪ Adm; free with Copenhagen Card ▪ www.roskildemuseum.dk

This museum illustrates Roskilde's history from the time when it was Denmark's first capital.

(4) Roskilde Kloster
MAP P6 ▪ Sankt Peders Straede 8E ▪ 46 35 02 19 ▪ www.roskilde kloster.dk

This manor was converted into a home for unmarried mothers.

(5) Skomagergade and Algade
MAP P6

The city's two main cobbled streets are lined with shops and cafés.

(6) Hestetorvet
MAP Q6

The Horse Market is set in what was Roskilde's largest square for centuries. Three giant vases commemorate Roskilde's millennium in 1998.

(7) Kirkegård
MAP Q6

Now a park, this former medieval churchyard holds the graves of many prominent Roskilde citizens.

(8) Stændertorvet
MAP P6 ▪ Markets on Wed & Sat

This small square in front of the Town Hall has been a marketplace since the Middle Ages.

(9) Roskilde Palace
MAP P6 ▪ Stændertorvet 3
▪ 46 31 65 70 ▪ Open noon–4pm Tue–Sun ▪ Adm for adults ▪ www.samtidskunst.dk

Built in 1733–6 for royal visitors, this yellow, four-wing Baroque building houses the country's first Museum of Contemporary Art.

(10) Musicon
Rabalderstræde 1 ▪ 46 31 68 68 ▪ www.musicon.dk

This council-run, former concrete factory is a buzz of creativity, with a dance theatre, skatepark, interactive playground, artists' studios, markets and regular events. It is also home to Ragnarock, the national museum of pop, rock and youth culture.

Artists at work outside Musicon

Louisiana Museum

Relaxing in the gardens of Louisiana Museum

1 Big Thumb (1968)
This striking, 2-m- (6-ft-) tall bronze thumb is modelled after the thumb of its creator, French sculptor César Baldaccini (1921–98).

2 Dead Drunk Danes (1960)
Rebel artist Asger Jorn (1914–73) was awarded the Guggenheim International Award for this expressive abstract painting. However, he rejected the accolade and sent Harry Guggenheim an infuriated telegram: "Go to hell with your money bastard *stop* Never asked for it *stop* Against all decency to mix artist against his will in your publicity *stop*".

3 A Closer Grand Canyon (1998)
This monumental, colourful work by David Hockney (1937–) is a series of small canvases pieced together.

4 Close Cover Before Striking (1962)
An early Andy Warhol acrylic painting in the Pop Art style.

5 Déjeuner sur l'Herbe (1961)
This abstract work by Pablo Picasso (1881–1973) pays homage to Edouard Manet's revolutionary painting of 1862–3, in which a nude woman sits in a classical setting, having a picnic with two clothed modern men.

6 Alberto Giacometti Collection
The museum owns an impressive collection of 13 sculptures and several drawings by Giacometti (1901–66). The elongated figures with rough textures are reminiscent of African sculpture.

7 Two Piece Reclining Figure No 5 (1963–4)
This bronze work by Henry Moore (1898–1986) occupies a beautiful spot between the trees, its humanoid, organic forms melding with the landscape.

8 Homage to the Square: Yellow Climate (1962)
This is part of the series titled *Homage to the Square* by Josef Albers (1888–1976), the Bauhaus artist who explored the chromatic relationship of different coloured flat squares.

9 Figures in a Landscape (1977)
In this painting by Roy Lichtenstein (1923–97), an exponent of Pop Art, symbols and images are broken down in a Cubist style.

10 The Sculpture Park
In the museum's sculpture park, the visual arts, architecture and landscapes exist in unity. The views are as much a part of the park's charm as its exhibits.

See map on p98

Helsingør

1 Maritime Museum of Denmark

MAP Q2 ■ Ny Kronborgvej 1 ■ 49 21 06 85 ■ Open Sep–Jun: 11am–5pm Tue–Sun; Jul–Aug: 10am–5pm daily ■ Adm; free with Copenhagen Card & for under-18s ■ www.mfs.dk

This interactive museum features hands-on digital exhibits.

2 Festivals

www.visitnordsjaelland.com

Helsingør's summer festivals include the Maritime Festival Baltic Sail, Sunset Jazz Festival in Hornbæk, and the Hamlet Festival each August.

3 Karmeliterklosteret

MAP P2 ■ Sankt Anna Gade 38 ■ 49 21 17 74 ■ Open 10am–2pm Tue–Sun ■ Adm ■ www.sctmariae.dk

The Carmelite Order owned this 15th-century Gothic-style monastery.

4 Helsingør Bymuseum

MAP P2 ■ Sankt Anna Gade 36 ■ 49 28 18 00 ■ Open noon–4pm Tue–Fri & Sun, 10am–2pm Sat ■ Adm; free with Copenhagen Card

The town museum was once a sailors' hospital. Exhibits recall its history and that of this medieval town.

5 Kronborg Slot

MAP Q2 ■ Kronborg 2C ■ 49 21 30 78 ■ Open 11am–4pm daily (Nov–Mar: closed Mon); Jun–Aug: 10am–5:30pm daily ■ Adm; free with Copenhagen Card ■ www. kongeligeslotte.dk

Known as the setting of Shakespeare's *Hamlet*, this castle (see p42) was built in 1420. Its Great Hall is the largest in Europe.

6 Axeltorv

MAP P2

This square features a statue of Erik of Pomerania, the Polish prince who ruled Denmark from 1397 to 1439.

7 Stengade and Strandgade

MAP P3 ■ www.helsingormuseer.dk

Stengade is a pedestrianized street in the medieval quarter. Some houses on the parallel Strandgade date back to the 1400s; No 91 is now the Museet Skibsklarerergaarden.

8 Sankt Olai Kirke (Helsingør Domkirke)

MAP P2 ■ Sankt Anna Gade 12 ■ 49 21 04 43 ■ Open May–Aug: 10am–4pm Mon–Fri; Sep–Apr: 10am–2pm) ■ www.helsingoerdomkirke.dk

Note the 15th-century crucifix, the 1568 Renaissance pulpit, the 1579 baptismal font and the carved wooden altar.

9 Danmarks Teknisk Museum

Fabriksvej 25 ■ 49 22 26 11 ■ Open 10am–5pm Tue–Sun ■ Adm for adults ■ www.tekniskmuseum.dk

The machines at this museum of science and technology include steam engines, cars and aeroplanes.

10 Øresundsakvariet

MAP P1 ■ Strandpromenaden 5 ■ 35 32 19 70 ■ Open Jun–Aug: 10am–5pm daily; Sep–May: 10am–4pm Mon–Fri, 10am–5pm Sat & Sun ■ Adm; free with Copenhagen Card

This small aquarium houses an impressive variety of tropical fish and Baltic species.

A yacht sailing past Kronborg Slot

Places to Eat

① Café Bomhuset
MAP B2 ▪ Skovriderkroen, Strandvejen 235, Charlottenlund ▪ 39 65 67 00 ▪ www.cafebomhuset. dk ▪ ⓀⓀ

An upscale alternative to the typical outdoor café. The terrace is popular.

② Café Jorden Rundt
MAP B2 ▪ Strandvejen 152, Charlottenlund ▪ 39 63 73 81 ▪ Ⓚ

This café offers great sea views from its panoramic windows. Popular for brunch, sandwiches and cakes.

③ Søllerød Kro
MAP B2
▪ Søllerødvej 35, Holte ▪ 45 80 25 05 ▪ Closed Mon–Tue ▪ www.soelleroed-kro.dk ▪ ⓀⓀⓀ

This Michelin-starred restaurant has set menus and à la carte dishes.

④ Den Gule Cottage
MAP B2 ▪ Strandvejen 506, Klampenborg ▪ 39 64 06 91 ▪ Closed mid-Feb–May & mid-Nov–mid-Dec: Mon–Wed; mid-Dec–mid-Feb ▪ www. dengulecottage.dk ▪ ⓀⓀ

This cottage was designed in 1844 by the great Danish architect Gottlieb Bindesbøll. Dishes are prepared with seasonal ingredients.

⑤ Mumm
MAP N6 ▪ Karen Oldsdatters Stræde 9, Roskilde ▪ 46 37 22 01 ▪ Dinner only; closed Sun ▪ ⓀⓀⓀ

On one of Roskilde's oldest streets, this upscale, tiny French-Danish restaurant has a pretty courtyard.

⑥ Restaurant Gilleleje Havn
MAP A1 ▪ Havnevej 14, Gilleleje ▪ 48 30 30 39 ▪ Closed Mon–Tue ▪ www.gillelejehavn.dk ▪ ⓀⓀ

Enjoy traditional Danish seafood at this old seamen's inn (1895).

⑦ Restaurant Sletten
MAP B2 ▪ Gl. Strandvej 137, Humlebæk ▪ 49 19 13 21 ▪ Closed Sep–May: Sun–Mon ▪ www.sletten.dk ▪ ⓀⓀ

Sletten serves excellent value French cuisine, with the bonus of a sea view.

The stylish interior of Den Røde Cottage

⑧ Den Røde Cottage
MAP B2 ▪ Strandvejen 550, Klampenborg ▪ 39 90 46 14 ▪ D only; closed Feb; Oct–Apr: Sun ▪ www. denroedecottage.dk ▪ ⓀⓀⓀ

The sophisticated sister to neighbouring Den Gule Cottage, Den Røde offers exquisite seasonal menus.

⑨ Snekken
MAP P4 ▪ Vindeboder 16, Roskilde ▪ 46 35 98 16 ▪ www. snekken.dk ▪ ⓀⓀ

Locals book a table at Snekken for contemporary cuisine and sea views.

⑩ Paustian
MAP B2 ▪ Kalkbrænderiløbskaj 2, Copenhagen ▪ 39 18 55 01 ▪ www. paustian.com ▪ ⓀⓀ

Attached to Paustian furniture house, the interiors here are unsurprisingly stunning. Gorgeous harbour views.

See map on p98

Streetsmart

Bicycles lined up outside a timber framed building in the old town

Getting To and Around Copenhagen

Arriving by Air

Airlines flying directly to **Copenhagen Airport** include **Scandinavian Airlines**, **British Airways**, **easyJet** and **Norwegian**. The airport is located in Kastrup, 12 km (7 miles) southeast of the city. It takes around 15 minutes to reach the city centre by train or Metro (the station is near Terminal 3), or 45 minutes by bus (both cost the same). You will also find a taxi rank just outside Terminal 3. Expect to pay around 300 Dkr for a cab to the city centre.

Arriving by Train

Copenhagen is connected by train to many European cities, including Hamburg, Berlin and Stockholm. All international trains stop at the large Københavns Hovedbanegård central station, part of **Danish State Railways** (DSB). If you plan to travel on to Sweden, be aware that when you travel you will have to disembark at Copenhagen Airport to have your passport or identity card checked before being allowed to cross the Øresund Bridge into Malmö.

Arriving by Road

If driving to Copenhagen from Sweden, you can take the **Øresund Bridge** from Malmö. If driving in from Germany and crossing the island of Funen, you can cross the **Great Belt Bridge** to Sjælland,

the island on which the city of Copenhagen lies. Both bridges exact a toll.

Arriving by Ferry

You can take a **Polferries** ferry from Swinoujscie in Poland, or a **DFDS Seaways** ferry from Oslo in Norway. There are no longer any direct ferry routes between the UK and Denmark.

Travelling by Public Transport

Arriva buses, DSB local trains and **Metro Service** rapid transit systems are fast and reliable, with certain routes running 24/7. You can take a bike for free onto S-trains (S-tog), but there are generally some restrictions on the Metro during peak hours. In Greater Copenhagen, you can use a single ticket or buy a **Rejsekort**, which is a prepaid smart card which can be topped up and used on all three systems. Smart cards work out cheaper than buying individual tickets, but you can only purchase them from stations. Most S-tog stations have a 7/11 convenience store which doubles as a ticket office.

Travelling by Harbour Bus

Harbour buses (991, 992, 993) run the length of the city's harbour between Nordre Toldbod (near the Gefionspringvandet fountain), past Den Sorte Diamant to Teglholmen,

south of Fisketorvet. They run from 7am to 7pm Monday to Friday, and from 10am Saturday to Sunday, roughly every 15 minutes at peak times, hourly at other times.

Travelling by Taxi and Rickshaw

Available taxis have a "fri" (free) sign on the roof, but hailing one can prove a challenge. It can often be quicker to find a taxi rank; most S-train and Metro stations will have one nearby. The biggest firms in Denmark are **TaxiNord** and **DanTaxi**; both offer a credit card payment option and receipts. **Uber** is also widespread. For an open-air ride, you can catch the cycle rickshaws for relatively short rides from Storkespringvandet, Tivoli, Rådhuspladsen and Nyhavn, but beware – this method of transport can be rather expensive.

Travelling by Car

You can drive in Denmark if you are over 18 and hold a valid licence. Always carry the registration papers and a reflecting triangle – and always watch out for cyclists. There are several good car share schemes in operation around the city, the most popular being **Drive Now** and LetsGo, which offer a very good, cost-effective way of travelling long distances with larger groups. In Copenhagen, on-street parking in the city centre can be a challenge, and car parks are expensive. There are many parking apps, including **Easypark**, **Parkman** or **Parkpark**, which use your mobile phone's GPS to pinpoint your spot, and also enable you to pay online using a credit card; often this is easier than trying to find a ticket machine. The street sign "Parkering forbudt" means no parking within certain time limits. Note that motoring offences attract on-the-spot fines.

Travelling by Bus and Boat

Enjoy the city at your own pace with the **Stromma** (see p13) hop-on-hop-off bus tour, which covers all the city's top tourist hot spots. Alternatively, you can explore Copenhagen's charming canals by boat. Tours depart from Nyhavn and Holmens Kanal, and you can choose either an hour-long grand tour or a hop-on-hop-off flexible day pass. Stromma, in Nyhavn, offers the biggest choice of tours, including some that have live music and on-board dining. **Netto Boats** (see p13), also located in Nyhavn, is a slightly cheaper but equally good alternative.

Travelling by Bicycle

Cycling is undoubtedly the best way to get around Copenhagen. The city boasts an unparalleled number of dedicated cycle paths, and bicycles can be rented for 30 Dkr per hour. While it is not mandatory to wear a helmet while cycling, it is certainly recommended, especially in the city centre. It is illegal to cycle at night without front and rear lights so make sure your rental bike is fitted with both; a bell can be handy, too. Free city bikes offered by **Bycyklen** are also available year-round from stands across the city, and include a built-in sat-nav system. You must register online before you can use them. Remember to stick to the cycle paths where available, and always stop to allow passengers onto and off buses.

Travelling on Foot

Copenhagen is compact and flat, making it a joy to explore on foot. Many of the sights, especially those in the city centre, are just a short walk away from one other. Make sure you don't confuse bike lanes with pedestrian pavements as this can be a painful mistake.

Practical Information

Passports and Visas

Visitors from outside the European Economic Area (EEA), European Union (EU) and Switzerland need a valid passport to travel to Denmark, as do UK visitors. Swiss, EEA and EU nationals can use identity cards instead. Visitors from Canada, the US, Australia and New Zealand can stay for up to 90 days without a visa, as long as their passport is valid for 6 months beyond the date of entry. A visa is necessary for longer stays and must be obtained in advance from the Danish embassy (Schengen visas are valid). All other visitors need valid passports and visas. The **Ministry of Foreign Affairs** has up-to-date details. Most countries have consular representation in Copenhagen, including **Australia**, the **UK**, **Canada** and the **US**.

Customs and Immigration

Denmark imposes strict limits on what can be imported. Do not carry food items that have not been vacuum-packed by the manufacturer. Items in commercial quantities and gifts valued at more than 1,350 Dkr are also subject to customs duty. US citizens are liable to pay duty if carrying goods worth more than $400.

Travel Safety Advice

Visitors can get up-to-date travel safety information from the **UK Foreign and Commonwealth Office**, the **US Department of State** and the **Australian Department of Foreign Affairs and Trade**.

Travel Insurance

Do not travel without valid insurance, and be sure to check the policy's details, particularly how much you can claim for the loss of individual items. If you require medical treatment you may have to pay and claim it back later.

Health

Tourists are covered by public health services if there is an agreement between Denmark and their home country. EU nationals should carry a valid **EHIC** (European Health Insurance Card). Emergency treatment is free, unless the hospital concludes that the emergency was the result of a pre-existing condition. **Rigshospitalet** is a good hospital for urgent care, while **Bispebjerg Hospital** has an A&E department. If you require emergency dental treatment, head to **Dentist Tandlægevagten**. Doctors' fee refunds can be obtained at the nearest municipal or health insurance office. Prescription medication can be bought at pharmacies (apotek), denoted by a green "A" sign. Credit cards are not accepted. **Steno Apotek** is open 24/7.

Personal Security

Copenhagen is a safe city, but visitors must take precautions. Make sure your credit cards, mobile phone and cash are kept in a safe place, and be wary of pickpockets on public transport, particularly on crowded Metro trains. If you are a victim of a crime, contact the **Central Police Station** to file a report. You will be given a crime report note, which you will need for any insurance claims.

Emergency Services

In a crisis situation, or if you witness a serious crime, call **emergency** services immediately.

Travellers With Specific Needs

Copenhagen is a relatively accessible city, although some shops and restaurants in the older parts of the city centre do not offer facilities for those with specific needs. While the city is almost completely flat, its cobblestone roads can be a challenge for wheelchairs. All public transport, however, is accessible. **DSB Handicap Service** has useful information on public transport accessibility, and the **Visit Copenhagen** office lists places that offer facilities for the disabled.

Travelling With Children

Several museums have children's facilities and exhibitions for younger visitors. Most restaurants provide high chairs and children's menus, but not all offer baby-changing facilities. The two major department stores, **ILLUM** (see p73) and **Magasin du Nord** (see pp22–3), have play and baby-changing areas. The airport has buggies for use in the terminal, and baby-changing and play areas. Prams can be taken on public transport for free (buses only have space for two at a time).

Currency and Banking

Denmark is not part of the eurozone, and while some shops will accept euros, the local currency (Danish kroner) is usually preferred. Danish notes come in denominations of 1,000 Dkr, 500 Dkr, 200 Dkr, 100 Dkr and 50 Dkr; while coins are 20 Dkr, 10 Dkr, 5 Dkr, 2 Dkr, 1 Dkr and 50 øre (half a krone). Banks open 10am to 10pm Monday to Wednesday and 10am to 6pm Thursday. Most ATMs are open 24/7, and are usually found outside banks and Metro stations. Using American Express, MasterCard or Visa cards is not a problem. Some smaller shops will only accept Dankort (a debit card only available to Danes), so it is best to always carry some cash. There are many exchange bureaux across the city; those open longest include the **Forex** (8am–9pm) at the central station and the **Danske Bank** exchange office (6am–10pm) at the airport. Many hotels exchange money, but the rate can be much lower than at official exchange bureaux.

Telephone and Internet

The international dialling code for Denmark is +45; there are no area codes. To make international calls from Denmark, first dial 00. Public telephones accept coins and phonecards. Insert 5–20 Dkr for international calls, but note you will not receive change. GSM-compatible mobile phones will work, and 4G network coverage is excellent in most of the city. The main service providers are **TDC**, **Telenor** and **Telia**. Check your service provider's roaming rates before you travel though. Most hotels offer internet access and Wi-Fi. Many trains and buses and some public spaces have free Wi-Fi.

DIRECTORY

PASSPORTS AND VISAS

Australia
Dampfaergevej 26
W denmark.embassy.gov.au

Canada
Kristen Bernikowsgade 1
W denmark.gc.ca

Ministry of Foreign Affairs
W um.dk/en

UK
Kastelsvej 36–40
W ukindenmark.fco.gov.uk

US
Dag Hammarskjölds Allé 24
W dk.usembassy.gov

TRAVEL SAFETY ADVICE

Australian Department of Foreign Affairs and Trade
W dfat.gov.au
W smartraveller.gov.au

UK Foreign and Commonwealth Office
W gov.uk/foreign-travel-advice

US Department of State
W travel.state.gov

HEALTH

Bispebjerg Hospital
W bispebjerghospital.dk

Dentist
Tandlægevagten
W dentalklinikken.dk

EHIC
W nhs.uk/ehic

Rigshospitalet
W rigshospitalet.dk

Steno Apotek
W stenoapotek.dk

PERSONAL SECURITY

Central Police Station
C 33 14 14 48

EMERGENCY SERVICES

Emergency
C 112/114

TRAVELLERS WITH SPECIFIC NEEDS

DSB Handicap Service
C 70 13 14 15

Visit Copenhagen
Vesterbrogade 4
W visitcopenhagen.com

CURRENCY AND BANKING

Danske Bank
W danskebank.com

Forex
W forexbank.dk/en

TELEPHONE AND INTERNET

TDC
C 70 70 30 30
W tdc.dk

Telenor
C 72 10 01 00
W telenor.dk

Telia
C 80 40 40 29
W telia.dk

Postal Services

Post offices are open 9 or 10am to 5:30pm Monday to Friday and 9am to noon Saturday. In the city centre, **Posthus Pilestræde** is a convenient post office; **Posthus Østerbro** is in Østerbro. International mail arrives faster with the Faste Deliver A-mail or Prioritaire mail service, but this can be expensive. Check the **PostNord** website for rates.

TV, Radio and Newspapers

Cable and satellite TV offer channels in English and other languages, and most of the US and UK programmes broadcast by Danish networks are in English with Danish subtitles. **DR Radio** does not broadcast current affairs in English, but it does update its website with the news in English. Denmark's national newspapers include **Politiken**, **Børsen**, and **Information**; for local news in English, pick up a copy of the **Copenhagen Post** (published Friday). You can find most major UK and US newspapers at the airport, central station and in some city centre kiosks. English news website thelocal.dk is useful for current events.

Opening Hours

Shops are open 9:30 or 10am to 5:30pm Monday to Thursday, 9:30 or 10am to 7 or 8pm Friday and 9:30 or 10am to 3pm Saturday (to 5pm on the first Saturday of the month). Since the trading laws have been relaxed, larger shops now open on Sundays. You may find weekend hours extended in tourist areas, especially during summer.

Time Difference

Copenhagen is on Central European Time (CET), which is an hour ahead of London, six hours ahead of New York, nine hours ahead of Los Angeles and eight hours behind Sydney.

Electrical Appliances

You can use your electric appliances in Denmark if the standard voltage in your country is in the range of 220–240 volts. If it is in the range of 100–127 volts (as in the US, Canada and most South American countries), you will need a voltage converter. Sockets take standard European double round-pin plugs, so you may also need to use a plug adaptor.

Driving

To hire a car you need to be over 20 years old and have held a full driving licence for at least a year. To pick up the car, you will need your passport and a credit card to pay the security deposit. You may also need an International Driving Permit (IDP).

Weather

Denmark has a rather temperate climate, with no extremes of heat or cold, but the weather can be very changeable. July and August are the two hottest and sunniest months in Copenhagen, with temperatures of 19° C (68° F), while the months of January and February are the coldest, with temperatures of 2° C (35° F). The best times to visit are the summer, when you can enjoy as many as 16–18 hours of daylight on clear days, and Christmas, which is when the concept of hygge really comes into its own. The only time you might want to avoid visiting – due to chilly winds and limited daylight hours (just 7) – is January.

Visitor Information

The **Visit Copenhagen** (see p111) tourist office is close to the central railway station and offers a wealth of visitor information, as well as hotel bookings, car hire, the **Copenhagen Card** and information about tours. The *Copenhagen Post* lists all the arts, music and cultural events taking place across the city, while Danish-speakers can check the Friday guide sections of daily newspapers *Politiken* and *Berlingske*. The **Visit Denmark**, **Copenhagen Tourist** and Visit Copenhagen websites are useful resources with plenty of information.

Shopping

What it lacks in size, the main shopping district makes up for in quality and variety. Few capitals can match the dizzying array of independent stores and high-end boutiques on offer, and the city centre also boasts two major department stores: **Magasin du Nord** (see pp22–3) and **ILLUM** *(see p73)*. The biggest stores are located on **Strøget** *(see p62)*, Europe's longest pedestrianized street. Shoppers should head to **Royal Copenhagen** *(see p73)* for exclusive porcelain, **Birger Christensen** *(see p73)* for high-end designer fashion and **Illums Bolighus** *(see p73)* for beautiful Danish-designed homewares.

Venturing off the beaten track is just as rewarding; **Kronprinsensgade** *(see p62)* in the city centre is great for Danish fashion and streetwear, while unique **Ravnsborggade** in Nørrebro is the perfect place for antique-hunting.

If malls are more your thing, hop on the Metro to **Field's** in Ørestaden, or take a ride on the S-tog to Dybbølsbro Station for **Fisketorvet Copenhagen Mall** *(see p62)*. Prices can often be eye-wateringly expensive, but there are frequent sales. Look out for signs saying *slutspurt*, *lagersalg* or *udsalg* to find good bargains.

Dining

You're spoilt for choice in terms of dining options in Copenhagen. The city is home to some of the best restaurants in the world, and while you may not find the same variety of international cuisine you would in, for example, London, it is difficult to find a poor-quality eatery.

Most restaurants will open for dinner at around 6pm, with kitchens typically closing at around 10 or 10:30pm. Booking is always strongly advised, especially if you're planning on dining out on

Friday and Saturday evenings, as eating out is one of the Danes' favourite things to do.

Most restaurants in the city are child-friendly, but families with babies and toddlers are advised to check ahead that high chairs and baby-changing facilities are available.

Menu prices are high, and it can often be difficult to find a reasonably priced bottle of wine, even in lower-priced restaurants. Look out for early bird deals, and if you're travelling in the month of February, take advantage of **Copenhagen Dining Week**, during which hundreds of restaurants across the city offer popular cut-price menus.

Accommodation

Copenhagen has a wide range of accommodation available, but be aware that it does not come cheap. Make sure you do your research and book well in advance. Weekend stays in hotels can be cheaper than weekdays. If money is not an issue, you'll find plenty of high-end hotels scattered across the city, the most exclusive being the popular five-star **Hotel d'Angleterre** *(see p114)*, which enjoys a prime location on Kongens Nytorv and boasts its own in-house spa.

A more affordable and often authentic option is to rent an apartment via **Airbnb** – you'll find thousands across the city. **Couchsurfing** is another popular way of meeting locals and staying in the city without spending a huge amount of money.

DIRECTORY

POSTAL SERVICES

Posthus Østerbro
Øster Allé 1
📞 70 70 70 30

Posthus Pilestræde
Pilestræde 58
📞 70 70 70 30

PostNord
🌐 postnord.com

TV, RADIO AND NEWSPAPERS

Børsen
🌐 børsen.dk

Copenhagen Post
🌐 cphpost.dk

DR Radio
🌐 dr.dk/radio

Information
🌐 information.dk

Politiken
🌐 politiken.dk

VISITOR INFORMATION

Berlingske
🌐 b.dk

Copenhagen Card
🌐 copenhagencard.com

Copenhagen Tourist
🌐 cph-tourist.dk

Visit Copenhagen
🌐 visitcopenhagen.com

Visit Denmark
🌐 denmark.dk

SHOPPING

Field's
🌐 fields.dk

Ravnsborggade
🌐 ravnsborggade.dk

DINING

Copenhagen Dining Week
🌐 diningweek.dk

ACCOMMODATION

Airbnb
🌐 airbnb.com

Couchsurfing
🌐 couchsurfing.com

Places to Stay

PRICE CATEGORIES
For a standard double room per night (with breakfast if included), taxes and extra charges.

(Kr) under 1,000 (Kr) (Kr) 1,000–1,600 (Kr) (Kr) (Kr) over 1,600

Luxury Hotels

Copenhagen Plaza
MAP G5 ▪
Bernstorffsgade 4 ▪ 33 14 92 62 ▪ www.ligula.se/ profilhotels/copenhagen-plaza ▪ (Kr) (Kr)
Built in 1913, this historic hotel has spacious rooms and traditional decor. The Library Bar, packed with 18th-century books, is one of the city's best spots for a nightcap.

Hotel Front
MAP L4 ▪ Skt Annæ Plads 21 ▪ 33 13 34 00 ▪ www. scandichotels.dk/front ▪ (Kr) (Kr)
Child-friendly boutique hotels can be hard to come by, but this place offers rooms of various sizes. Each room has been uniquely decorated and enhanced with attractive artwork.

Hotel Alexandra
MAP G5 ▪ H C Andersens Boulevard 8 ▪ 33 74 44 44 ▪ www.hotelalexandra.dk ▪ (Kr) (Kr) (Kr)
This excellent hotel has been around for more than a century and is popular for its original, 20th-century furniture, with design classics ranging from Kaare Klint chairs to some bespoke Akademi chandeliers designed by artist Poul Henningsen. There are three non-smoking floors as well as a selection of allergy-tested rooms.

Hotel d'Angleterre
MAP K4 ▪ Kongens Nytorv 34 ▪ 33 12 00 95 ▪ www. dangleterre.dk ▪ (Kr) (Kr) (Kr)
Olden-day grandeur meets modern luxury at this hotel. It has a plush palm court, banquet rooms, a spa and an elegant restaurant.

Nimb Hotel
MAP G5 ▪ Bernstorffsgade 5 ▪ 88 70 00 00 ▪ www. nimb.dk ▪ (Kr) (Kr) (Kr)
The most exclusive hotel in Copenhagen has just 21 rooms. Each one is unique and luxurious, and features range from open fireplaces to flatscreen TVs. Housed in the landmark Nimb building, and with its own private limousine service, this is A-list accommodation.

Nyhavn 71
MAP L4 ▪ Nyhavn 71 ▪ 33 43 62 00 ▪ www. 71nyhavnhotel.com ▪ (Kr) (Kr) (Kr)
This charming four-star hotel was once a warehouse built to store goods from ships in the harbour. The area is very peaceful as it's not well-known to tourists in the city.

Palace Hotel
MAP H5 ▪ Rådhuspladsen 57 ▪ 33 14 40 50 ▪ www. scandichotels.com/ hotels/denmark/ copenhagen/scandic-palace ▪ (Kr) (Kr) (Kr)
Rooms at this Victorian hotel are decorated in an English style but have a modern twist. Celebrities like Judy Garland, Audrey Hepburn and Errol Flynn have added a touch of glamour to the hotel.

Sankt Petri
MAP H4 ▪ Krystalgade 22 ▪ 33 45 91 00 ▪ www. sktpetri.com ▪ (Kr) (Kr) (Kr)
Every room of this lovely five-star hotel is delightfully decorated with orchids and abstract art, and the bathrooms are gorgeous. It has a popular glass-roofed atrium which often features international DJs. It also has a cocktail bar.

Boutique Hotels

Avenue Hotel
MAP C4 ▪ Åboulevard 29 ▪ 35 37 31 11 ▪ www. brochner-hotels.dk/hotel-avenue-copenhagen ▪ (Kr) (Kr)
This boutique hotel is on the edge of Frederiksberg, close to both the Lakes and the lively Nørrebro district. A hotel since 1939, it offers child-friendly, spacious family rooms. Breakfast can be enjoyed on the terrace, which has a child's sandpit.

Babette Guldsmeden
MAP L2 ▪ Bredgade 78 ▪ 33 48 10 00 ▪ www. guldsmedenhotels.dk ▪ (Kr) (Kr)
In a very peaceful location close to the green area of Kastellet (see p80), this green-certified hotel is inside a 19th-century building. Services include free organic coffee and there is also a rather useful 24-hour snack bar.

Hotel SP34

MAP G4 ▪ Sankt Peders Stræde 34 ▪ 33 13 30 00 ▪ www.brochner-hotels. dk ▪ Ⓚ Ⓚ

This stylish boutique hotel is located in the Latin Quarter, not far from Rådhuspladsen. There are 118 beautifully furnished rooms, all with free Wi-Fi and cable TV. The hotel has two good restaurants, a lounge bar, a café and a terrace.

Imperial Hotel

MAP G5 ▪ Vester Farimagsgade 9 ▪ 33 12 80 00 ▪ www.imperial-hotel-copenhagen.com ▪ Ⓚ Ⓚ

Stylish and welcoming, this four-star hotel has been decorated in modern Danish design and has an entire floor dedicated to the work of late Danish designer Børge Mogensen.

Hotel Sanders

MAP K4 ▪ Tordenskjoldsgade 15 ▪ 70 20 28 18 ▪ www. hotelsanders.com ▪ Ⓚ Ⓚ Ⓚ

This five-storey luxury boutique hotel is housed in a Jugendstil building from the 1860s. Rooms range from snug to very spacious. The magnificent interior features bespoke Colonial furniture and Danish classic design.

Hotel Twentyseven

MAP H5 ▪ Løngangstræde 27 ▪ 70 27 56 27 ▪ www. firsthotels.com ▪ Ⓚ Ⓚ Ⓚ

This boutique hotel, with its minimalist decor, is centrally located not far from Rådhuspladsen and Strøget. The hotel bars include a wine bar, a cocktail lounge and the Icebar Copenhagen.

Mid-Range Hotels

Savoy

MAP C5 ▪ Vesterbrogade 34 ▪ 33 26 75 00 ▪ www. savoyhotel.dk ▪ Ⓚ

Dating from 1906, this 66-room hotel is known for its distinctive Art Nouveau façade, and is a Vesterbro landmark. Renovated but still affordably priced, it has Wi-Fi connection in all rooms and a guest PC in the lobby. The rooms facing the courtyard are much quieter.

Axel Hotel Guldsmeden

MAP G6 ▪ Helgolandsgade 11 ▪ 33 31 32 66 ▪ www. hotelguldsmeden.dk ▪ Ⓚ Ⓚ

This boutique eco-hotel is a surprising find close to the main train station. Relax in the saunas and steam baths of the hotel spa and enjoy excellent organic breakfasts in the heated courtyard.

Carlton 66 Guldsmeden

MAP C5 ▪ Vesterbrogade 66 ▪ 33 22 15 00 ▪ www. hotelguldsmeden.dk ▪ Ⓚ Ⓚ

Sophisticated yet relaxed, this hotel has an ethnic decor with dark-wood furniture, whitewashed walls and Egyptian cotton sheets. It offers delicious organic breakfasts.

Ibsens Hotel

MAP G3 ▪ Vendersgade 23 ▪ 33 13 19 13 ▪ www. arthurhotels.dk/ibsens-hotel ▪ Ⓚ Ⓚ

This boutique hotel is in the Nansensgade area of the city, a short walk from Nørreport station. All rooms are individually decorated and there is a beautiful courtyard, too.

Manon Les Suites

MAP G4 ▪ Gyldenløvesgade 19 ▪ 45 70 00 15 ▪ www. guldsmedenhotels.com/ manon-les-suites ▪ Ⓚ Ⓚ

Manon offers 82 suites, each ideal for a family or five people. The hotel emphasizes sustainability, from daily operations to organic food and beauty products. Room decor is distinctly hip with a mid-century modern flavour.

The Square

MAP H5 ▪ Rådhuspladsen 14 ▪ 33 38 12 00 ▪ www. thesquarecopenhagen. com ▪ Ⓚ Ⓚ

This three-star hotel is located on the Town Hall square. It comes with stylish pony-hair chairs at the entrance and Arne Jacobsen chairs in the reception area. The breakfast is excellent.

First Hotel Mayfair

MAP G6 ▪ Helgolandsgade 3 ▪ 70 12 17 00 ▪ www. firsthotels.com ▪ Ⓚ Ⓚ Ⓚ

Close to the city's main attractions, this hotel is furnished mainly in an English style with a hint of the Oriental.

Tivoli Hotel

MAP D6 ▪ Arni Magnussons Gade 2 ▪ 44 87 00 00 ▪ www. tivolihotel.com ▪ Ⓚ Ⓚ Ⓚ

This high-rise hotel has activities for kids, as well as a pool and fitness centre. Part of the Tivoli Congress Center, it also caters for business guests. A free shuttle bus operates between the hotel and Tivoli.

Rooms with a View

Danhostel Copenhagen City
MAP J6 ▪ H C Andersens Blvd 50 ▪ 33 11 85 85 ▪ www.danhostel.dk/copenhagencity ▪ (Kr)
This modern and design-led Danhostel is one of the biggest in the city. It is located close to Tivoli and Rådhuspladsen.

Dragør Badehotel
MAP C3 ▪ Drogdensvej 43, Dragør ▪ 32 53 05 00 ▪ www.badehotellet.dk ▪ (Kr)
The fishing village of Dragør is a popular destination with tourists and this hotel's rooms have good views of the sea and the countryside.

Admiral
MAP L3 ▪ Toldbodgade 24–8 ▪ 33 74 14 14 ▪ www.admiralhotel.dk ▪ (Kr)(Kr)
Originally an 18th-century granary, this splendid four-star hotel has rooms offering stunning views of the Operaen (see pp94–5). The foyer displays models of ships. The restaurant, Salt, is excellent.

Copenhagen Island
MAP J6 ▪ Kalvebod Brygge 53 ▪ 33 38 96 00 ▪ www.copenhagenisland.com ▪ (Kr)(Kr)
This beautiful state-of-the-art hotel is on an island in the middle of Copenhagen harbour. Architect Kim Utzon's extraordinary building places a great emphasis on the play of glass and light. The rooms offer scenic views of the Sound. It also has its own, very well-equipped gym and fitness centre.

Copenhagen Strand
MAP L4 ▪ Havnegade 37 ▪ 33 48 99 00 ▪ www.copenhagenstrand.com ▪ (Kr)(Kr)
This three-star hotel is housed in a lovely 1869 harbourfront warehouse, tucked away on a pretty, quiet street opposite the Christianshavns canal. The decor is rustic and the view is wonderful.

Skodsborg Kurhotel and Spa
MAP B2 ▪ Skodsborg Strandvej 139, Skodsborg ▪ 45 58 58 00 ▪ www.skodsborg.dk ▪ (Kr)(Kr)
Once a summer palace, this century-old health resort is a beautiful place to stay. Overlooking the sea, it is the perfect destination for health and fitness fanatics, offering a good range of therapies and fitness programmes, plus healthy food.

Skovshoved Hotel
MAP B2 ▪ Strandvejen 267, Charlottenlund ▪ 39 64 00 28 ▪ www.skovshovedhotel.dk ▪ (Kr)(Kr)
Away from the bustle of central Copenhagen, this elegant seaside hotel is over 350 years old. Tastefully decorated in a Scandinavian style, it is surrounded by fishermen's houses and offers beautiful views. The restaurant is mentioned in the Michelin Guide, so be sure to book ahead.

Hotel CPHLIVING
MAP J6 ▪ Langebrogade 1C ▪ 61 60 85 46 ▪ www.cphliving.com ▪ (Kr)(Kr)(Kr)
The world's first floating hotel is located in a boat on the harbour. There are 12 rooms, all with small balconies and Wi-Fi. A sundeck with deck chairs is available for guests.

Radisson Blu Royal Hotel
MAP G5 ▪ Hammerichsgade 1 ▪ 33 42 60 00 ▪ www.radisson.com ▪ (Kr)(Kr)(Kr)
This famous Radisson hotel, designed by Arne Jacobsen in the 1950s, is packed with five-star comforts. The rooms afford great views over the city. Café Royal on the 20th floor serves high-end cuisine and afternooon tea.

Budget Hotels

CabInn City
MAP H6 ▪ Mitchellsgade 14 ▪ 33 46 16 16 ▪ www.cabinn.com ▪ (Kr)
Based on the idea of a ship's cabin, the rooms at CabInn City are small but perfectly designed, with all the modern conveniences tucked into a clever storage design. You can pick from bunk beds in twin rooms, double rooms and family rooms. The hotel has a pleasant ambience and every morning there is a very good buffet breakfast.

CabInn Metro
MAP H6 ▪ Arne Jakobsens Allé 2 ▪ 32 46 57 00 ▪ www.cabinn.com ▪ (Kr)
The Metro is the fourth hotel in the city's budget Cab Inn concept, and is Denmark's largest hotel. It is located very close to the city's airport and Field's shopping centre. All 710 rooms are modern and clean, and all have en-suite facilities. Free Wi-Fi access is always included in the room rate.

CabInn Scandinavia

MAP C4 ■ Vodroffsvej 55, Frederiksberg ■ 35 36 11 11 ■ www.cabinn.com ■ (Kr)

This CabInn hotel is located just a block away from the CabInn Express and a road before the Peblinge Lake. It is equipped with all the modern conveniences found at the other three CabInns in the city.

Generator Hostel Copenhagen

MAP K3 ■ Adelgade 5–7 ■ 78 77 54 00 ■ www. generatorhostels.com ■ (Kr)

A smart, modern hostel with private, en-suite rooms as well as dorms. Facilities include Wi-Fi, a bar and breakfast (for an extra charge).

Hotel Copenhagen

MAP E6 ■ Egilsgade 33, Islands Brygge ■ 32 96 27 27 ■ www.hotel copenhagen.dk ■ (Kr)

Just a few minutes away from the city centre by Metro, this hotel offers rooms sleeping up to four with shared bathrooms. There are also some very nice rooms with en-suite facilities. Free Wi-Fi is available in the reception and, for a small charge, a breakfast can be ordered when you book.

Wakeup Copenhagen Borgergade

MAP K3 ■ Borgergade 9 ■ 44 80 00 00 ■ www. wakeupcopenhagen.dk ■ (Kr)

This 498-room hotel ... odern ... on just ... Kongens ... nborg and

other city-centre sights. The interior is extremely stylish and part of a new generation of budget accommodation appearing in the city.

WakeUp Copenhagen Carsten Niebuhrs

MAP D6 ■ Carsten Niebuhrs Gade 11 ■ 44 80 00 10 ■ www.wakeup copenhagen.dk ■ (Kr)

Designed by Kim Utzon, this ultramodern, two-star budget hotel is located along the waterfront, close to Fisketorvet shopping mall. Its 510 rooms are spread over 12 floors, with prices rising per floor.

Other Accommodation

City Camp

Havneholmen 2 ■ 21 42 53 84 ■ Open May–1 Sep ■ www.citycamp.dk ■ (Kr)

Centrally located and close to the harbour, this is a good option if you want to park your camper van or caravan while in the city. To make reservations via email you will need to provide your vehicle's licence plate number and your arrival and departure dates.

Copenhagen Downtown Hostel

MAP J5 ■ Vandkunsten 5 ■ 70 23 21 10 ■ www. copenhagendowntown. com ■ (Kr)

Located right in the heart of the city, this hostel promises a vibrant and artistic international atmosphere. It has a café, lounge and restaurant. In addition to the dorm and four-bedded rooms, there are rooms for two

to three people with en-suite facilities. A YHA membership card is required, but this can be purchased when checking in.

Steel House Copenhagen

MAP C5 ■ Herholdtsgade 6 ■ 33 17 71 10 ■ www. steelhousecopenhagen. com ■ (Kr)

This 253-room hostel, opened in summer 2017, is a stone's throw from the Vesterport Station. Sleek rooms range from 6- and 4-bed dorms to single rooms. In addition to a self-service kitchen and cool craft-beer bar, there are sports facilities, a café, reading lounge, business centre, pool and music venue.

Apartment in Copenhagen

MAP E4 ■ Hindegade 6 ■ 77 34 56 45 ■ www. apartmentincopenhagen. com ■ (Kr)(Kr)

Agency specializing in short- and long-term lets in smart, furnished apartments at attractive city locations, for couples and for families.

STAY Apartment Hotel

MAP D6 ■ Islands Brygge 79A ■ 72 44 44 34 ■ www.staycopenhagen. dk ■ (Kr)(Kr)(Kr)

A stunning-looking building renovated by the designers of Hay House (see p73), STAY offers serviced apartments with superb waterfront views. The building also hous... excellent small h... restaurant, an ... supermarket ... good gourme...

General Index

Acknowledgments

Author
Antonia Cunningham

Additional contributor
Chris Moss

Publishing Director Georgina Dee
Publisher Vivien Antwi
Design Director Phil Ormerod
Editorial Ankita Awasthi Tröger, Rachel Fox, Maresa Manara, Alison McGill, Lucy Richards, Sally Schafer, Hollie Teague
Cover Design Richard Czapnik
Design Tessa Bindloss, Bharti Karakoti
Picture Research Susie Peachey, Ellen Root, Lucy Sienkowska
Cartography Subhashree Bharati, Suresh Kumar, Casper Morris
DTP Jason Little
Production Luca Bazzoli
Factchecker Taraneh Jerven
Proofreader Kathryn Glendenning
Indexer Hilary Bird

Picture Credits
The publisher would like to thank the following for their kind permission to reproduce their photographs:
Key: a-above; b-below/bottom; c-centre; f-far; l-left; r-right; t-top

108: Freya Mcomish 97cra.

123RF.com: bloodua 12bl; Oliver Förstner 87br; Chon Kit Leong 78bc; scanrail 23tl, 68tl; Figurniy Sergey 80cla.

Alamy Stock Photo: Arco Images / Di Rosa, G. 22bl; Jon Bilous 4cla; Richard Cummins 32–3; Directphoto Collection 30cra; Entertainment Pictures 47tr; Greg Balfour Evans 4clb; Oliver Förstner 98cla; Hemis / Bertrand Gardel 32bl; imageBROKER / NielsDK 19tl; John Peter Photography 93tl; Heini Kettunen 78t; Paul Maguire 4cl; Martin Norris Travel Photography 3tr, 106–107; Graham Mulrooney 1; Kim Petersen 42bl; Niels Poulsen mus 70tr; Niels Quist 28br, 96br; Realimage 20–21; Jani Riekkinen 4crb; Jonathan Smith 33crb; VWPics 57cl.

...urum: 96ca.

...kkehusmuseet: 46br, 89cl.

...rken Kbh: Polina Vinogradova 56br.

...aurant BROR: Gab Studio 75ca.

...hagen Media Center: Klaus Bentzen ...Vallmans Cirkusbygningen 54; ...agen Jazz Festival / Jonas Pryner ...Røde Cottage 105cr; Rasmus Flindt ...75br; Restaurant Kong Hans ...cl; Johan Rosenmunthe 88tr; Ty ...65cla; Strömma Danmark 72br;

Ulf Svane / The Spoon Company 65tr; Torvehallerne Kbh 63cl.

Copenhagen Pride Festival: Anders Jung 59tr.

Danish Royal Palaces: Thomas Rahbek 101cl, 104b.

Den Blå Planet: Bjarke MacCarthy 53cra, 100tl.

Designer Zoo: 90t.

Designmuseum Danmark: Pernille Klemp 76tl.

DR Koncerthuset: David Borland Architectural Photography 55cl.

Dreamstime.com: Albo 11b; Anderm 41cl; Andrey Andronov 38t; Leonid Andronov 16bl, 18–19, 70–71; Aurinko 24cl, 39cra, 80br; Jon Bilous 29tl; Bloodua 10tl; Collette Branco 69tl; Dennis Dolkens 77br; Michal Durinik 41tr; Igor Dymov 94bl; Eugenephoen 6tr, 42t; Oliver Förstner 10clb, 19crb, 51crb; Gary718 7br; Dennis Jacobsen 38bl; Kkllggnn 43cl; Irina Lepneva 12–13; Mapics 6cla; Marinv 62b; Sophie Mcaulay 77tr; Jaroslav Moravcik 48–9; Ohmaymay 4b; Pavel Parmenov 50b; Pod666 25tl; Rndmst 72tc; Natalia Rumyantseva 18br, Igor Stojakovic 13crb, Parinya Suwanitch 22–3; Jason Vosper 46tl; Vvoevale 10bl; Zastavkin 11cr, 28cl, 40tl.

Fisketorv Shopping Centre: 62tr.

Formel B: 60bc.

Getty Images: APIC 37tr; Cultura RM Exclusive / Atli Mar Hafsteinsson 87tl; DEA / G. Nimatallah 37cl, / A. Dagli Orti 36b, / G. Roli 36ca; Tim Graham 58–9; Annapurna Mellor 48tl; MyLoupe 45tr, /Universal Images Group 4cra.

iStockphoto.com: fotoVoyager 4t; krugli 93b; scanrail 2tl, 8–9; SeanPavonePhoto 3tl, 66–7.

The Jane: 56t.

Jazzhus Monmartre: Lars Gundersen 74t.

Georg Jensen AS, Denmark: Peter Krasilnikoff 63tr.

Kiin Kiin: 60t.

Kulturcentret Assistens: 47cl.

The Laundromat Cafe: 61tr.

Les Trois Cochons: Chris Tonnesen 91br.

Loppen: 29crb.

Louisiana Museum of Modern Art : Kim Hansen 103t.

Masken Bar & Café: 58tr.

Mikkeller: Theis Mortensen 50tl.

The Museum of National History at Frederiksborg Castle: 40–41, 100b; Mikkel Grønlund 84–5.

Musicon: Kim Wendt 102br.

Nationalmuseet, Danmark: Roberto Fortuna and Kira Ursem 11clb, 31br; Lennart Larsen 30br; John Lee 31tr.

Normann Copenhagen: Jeppe Sørensen 81tr.

North Atlantic House: 94tr.

Ny Carlsberg Glyptotek: Ana Cecilia Gonzalez 2tr, 34–5, 44b.

Orangeriet Kongens Have: 83cla.

Ordrupgaard: Anders Sune Berg 99br.

Ripley Entertainment Inc: Copenhagen Guinness World Records Museum / Johanne Lerbech 52bl.

Royal Copenhagen Porcelain: Gab Admin 73cb.

The Royal Danish Theatre: Christophe Pelc 54b; Costin Radu 23crb; Egon Street 95cl.

Rust: 82b.

Statens Museum for Kunst: 11cra, 26cla, 26br, 27tr, 45cl, 79cl.

Sticks 'n' Sushi: 91ca.

SuperStock: Yadid Levy 73cra.

Team Bade / Islands Brygge Harbour Bath: 13tl, 49tr.

The Danish Jewish Museum: 33tl; Joséfine Amalie 44tl.

The Royal Danish Collection: 17cr, 24cra; Iben Bolling Kaufmann 10crb, 16crb, 43br; Peter Norby 16–17, 17tl; Peter Nørby 11tl, 25crb, 25br.

Tivoli: Anders Bøggild 10c, 52t; Rasmus B. Hansen 15tl; Lasse Salling 14cla, 14bl, 14 -15, 15br; Tivoli Gardens / Lasse Salling 69crb.

The Viking Ship Museum, Denmark: Werner Karrasch 99t, 102cla.

WarPigs Brewpub: Camilla Stephan & Rasmus Malmstr 57tr.

Zoologisk Have: Frank Ronsholt 49cl, 86cla; Frank Rønsholt 88b.

Cover

Front and spine: **4Corners:** Maurizio Rellini
Back: **123RF.com:** Mikhail Markovskiy

Pull Out Map Cover
4Corners: Maurizio Rellini

All other images © Dorling Kindersley
For further information see:
www.dkimages.com

Penguin
Random
House

Printed and bound in China

First published in Great Britain in 2007
by Dorling Kindersley Limited
80 Strand, London WC2R 0RL

Copyright 2007, 2018 © Dorling
Kindersley Limited

A Penguin Random House Company

18 19 20 21 10 9 8 7 6 5 4 3 2 1

**Reprinted with revisions 2009, 2011,
2013, 2015, 2018**

ISBN 978 0 2412 9627 1

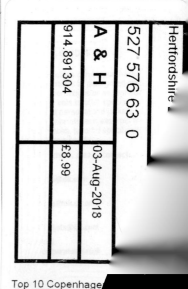

*As a guide to abbreviations in visitor information
blocks:* **Adm** = *admission charge;* **D** = *dinner;*
L = *lunch.*

Phrase Book

In an Emergency

Help!	Hjælp!	yellb!
Stop!	Stands!	stanns!
Can you call a doctor?	Kan du ringe til en læge?	kann do ringe-til ehn laiyeh?
Can you call an ambulance?	Kan du ringe til en ambulance?	kann do ringe-til ehn ahm-boo-lang-seh?
Can you call the police?	Kan du ringe til politiet?	kann do ringe-til po-ly-tee'd?
Can you call the fire brigade?	Kan du ringe til brand-væsenet?	kann do ringe-til brahn-vaiys-ned?
Is there a telephone here?	Er der en telefon i nærheden?	e-ah dah ehn tele-fohn ee neya-hethen?
Where is the nearest hospital?	Hvor er det nærmeste hospital?	voa e-ah deh neh-meste hoh-spee-tahl

Useful Phrases

Sorry	Undskyld	ons-gull
Goodnight	Godnat	goh-nad
Goodbye	Farvel	fah-vell
Good evening	Godaften	goh-ahf-tehn
Good morning	Godmorgen	goh-moh'n
Good day (after about 9am)	Goddag	goh-dah
Yes	Ja	yah
No	Nej	nye
Please	Værsgo/ Velbekomme	vehs-goh/ vell-beh-commeh
Thank you	Tak	tahgg
How are you?	Hvordan har du det?/ Hvordan går det?	voh-dann hah do deh?/ voh-dan go deh?
Well, thank you	Godt, tak	gohd, tahgg
Pleased to have met you	Det var rart at møde dig	deh vah rahd add meutheh die
See you!	Vi ses!	vee sehs!
I understand	Jeg forstår	yay fuh-stoah
I don't understand	Jeg forstår ikke	yay fuh-stoah egge
Does anyone speak English?	Er der nogen, der kan tale engelsk?	e-ah dah noh-enn dah kann tah-leh eng-ellsgg?
god	guth
dårlig	doh-lee
op	ohb
ned	neth
tæt på	taid poh
langt fra	lahngd fra
til venstre	till vehn-streh
til højre	till hoy-reh
åben	oh-ben
lukket	luh-geth
varm	vahm
kold	koll
stor	stoah
le	lee-leh

Making a Telephone Call

Whom am I speaking to?	Hvem taler jeg med?	vemm talah yay meth?
I would like to call…	Jeg vil gerne ringe til…	yay vill geh-neh ring-eh till…
I will telephone again	Jeg ringer en gang til	yay ring-ah ehn gahng till

In a Hotel

Do you have double rooms?	Findes her dobbelt-værelser?	feh-ness he-ah dob-belld vah-hel-sah?
With bathroom	Med bade-værelse	meth bah-the-vah-hel-sah
With washbasin	Med hånd-vask	meth hohn-vasgg
key	nøgle	noy-leh
I have a reservation	Jeg har en reservation	yay hah ehn res-sah-vah-shohn

Sightseeing

entrance	indgang	ehn-gahng
exit	udgang	ooth-gahng
exhibition	udstilling	ooth-stelling
tourist information	turisto-plysning	tooh-reesd-ohb-lehs-ning
town/city hall	rådhus	rahd-hus
post office	posthus	posd-hus
cathedral	domkirke	dom-kia-keh
church	kirke	kia-keh
museum	museum	muh-seh-uhm
town bus	bybus	bih-boos
long-distance bus	rutebil	bus roo-teh-beel
railway station	banegård	bah-neh-goh
airport	lufthavn	luhft-havn
train	tog	toh
ferry terminal	færgehavn	fah-veh-havn
bus stop	busstoppested	buhs-sdob-beh-steth
long-distance bus station	rutebilstation	roo-teh-beel-sta-shion
a public toilet	et offentligt toilet	ehd off-end-ligd toa-led

Shopping

I wish to buy…	Jeg vil gerne købe…	yay vill geh-neh kyh-beh…
Do you have…?	Findes der…?	feh-ness de-ah…?
How much does it cost?	Hvad koster det?	vath koh-stah deh
expensive	dyr	dyh-ah
cheap	billig	billy
size	størrelse	stoh-ell-seh
general store	købmand	keuhb-mann
greengrocer	grønthandler	grund-handla
supermarket	supermarked	suh-pah-mah-keth
market	marked	mah-keth

Eating Out

Do you have a table for… people?	Har I et bord til… personer?	hah ee ed boah till… peh-soh-nah?
I would like to sit by the window	Jeg vil gerne sidde ved vinduet	yay vill geh-neh saithe veth veen-do-ed

I wish to order...	**Jeg vil gerne bestille...**	yay vill geh-neh beh-stilleh...
I'm a vegetarian	**Jeg er vegetar**	yay eh-ah veh-gehta
children's menu	**børnemenu**	byeh-neh-meh-nye
daily special	**dagens ret**	dayens rad
starter	**forret**	foh-red
main course	**hovedret**	hoh-veth-red
dessert	**dessert**	deh-sehld
wine list	**vinkort**	veen-cod
sweet	**sødt**	sodt
sour	**surt**	suad
spicy	**stærkt**	stehgd
May I have the bill?	**Må jeg bede om regningen?**	moh yay beh-theh uhm rahy-ning-ehn

Menu Decoder

agurk	a-guag	cucumber
ananas	a-nah-nas	pineapple
appelsin	abbel-seen	orange
blomme	blum-ma	plum
brød	bruh	bread
champignon	sham-pee-ong	mushroom
danskvand	dansg vann	mineral water
fersken	fes-gehn	peach
fisk	fesgg	fish
fløde	flu-thoh	cream
gulerod	gooleh-roth	carrot
grøntsager	grunn-saha	vegetables
hummer	humma	lobster
is	ees	ice cream
kaffe	kah-feh	coffee
kartofler	kah-toff-luh	potatoes
kød	kuth	meat
kylling	killing	chicken
kål	kohl	cabbage
laks	lahggs	salmon
lam	lahm	lamb
leverpostej	leh-vah-poh-stie	liver paté
løg	loy	onion
mælk	mailgg	milk
oksekød	ogg-seh-kuth	beef
ost	ossd	cheese
peber	peh-ba	pepper
pore	po-a	leek
purløj	poo-a-loy	chives
pølse	pill-seh	sausage
rejer	rah-yah	shrimps
ris	rees	rice
rødspætte	roth-speh-da	plaice
røget fisk	roy-heth fesgg	smoked fish
saftevand	sah-fteh-vann	squash
salat	sah-lad	salad
salt	sald	salt
sild	sil	herring
skaldyr	sgall-dya	shellfish
skinke	sgeng-geh	ham
smør	smuah	butter
sodavand	sodah-vann	fizzy drink
steg	stie	steak
svinekød	svee-neh-kuth	pork
syltetøj	sill-teh-toi	jam
te	teh	tea
tærte	te-ah-teh	quiche/pie
torsk	tohsgg	cod
vand	vann	water

wienerbrød	vee-nah-bryd	Danish pastry
æble	eh-bleh	apple
æg	egg	egg
øl	uhl	beer

Time

today	**i dag**	ee-day
tomorrow	**i morgen**	ee-mohn
yesterday	**i går**	ee-goh
before noon	**formiddag**	foh-medday
afternoon	**eftermiddag**	ehftah-medday
evening	**aften**	ahftehn
night	**nat**	nadd
minute	**minut**	meh-nude
hour	**time**	tee-meh
week	**uge**	oo-eh
month	**måned**	moe-neth
year	**år**	oah

Days of the Week

Monday	**mandag**	mann-day
Tuesday	**tirsdag**	teahs-day
Wednesday	**onsdag**	uns-day
Thursday	**torsdag**	toahs day
Friday	**fredag**	frey day
Saturday	**lørdag**	lur-day
Sunday	**søndag**	son-day

Months

January	**januar**	ya-nuah
February	**februar**	fib-buah
March	**marts**	mahds
April	**april**	apreal
May	**maj**	mai
June	**juni**	yoo-nee
July	**juli**	yoo-lee
August	**august**	auw-guhsd
September	**september**	sehb-tern-bah
October	**oktober**	ogg-toh-bah
November	**november**	noh-vem-bah
December	**december**	deh-sem-bah

Numbers

0	**nul**	noll
1	**en**	ehn
2	**to**	toh
3	**tre**	tray
4	**fire**	fee-ah
5	**fem**	femm
6	**seks**	seggs
7	**syv**	siu
8	**otte**	oh-deh
9	**ni**	nee
10	**ti**	tee
20	**tyve**	tyh-veh
30	**tredive**	traith-veh
40	**fyrre**	fyr-reh
50	**halvtreds**	hahl-traiths
60	**tres**	traiths
70	**halvfjerds**	hahl-fyads
80	**firs**	fee-ahs
90	**halvfems**	hahl-femms
100	**hundrede**	huon-dreh-the
200	**tohundrede**	toh-hoon-dreh-the
1,000	**tusind**	tooh-sin-deh
2,000	**totusinde**	toh-tooh-sin-deh

Selected Copenhagen Street Index